AF655329

A TEXTBOOK OF
COMMUNICATION SKILL

About the Author

Mudassar Nazar Baidya has been serving as an Assistant Professor and Head in the Department of Education at Udaynarayanpur Madhabilata Mahavidyalaya, located in the Howrah district of West Bengal, India, since January 2017. He has published 20 research articles in various peer-reviewed journals, esteemed magazines, and reputed edited books. Additionally, he has presented 25 research papers at various international, national, state, and college-level seminars, conferences, and webinars, including two papers as a resource person. Furthermore, he has authored several books, such as *Nari Shiksha, Janosankhya Shiksha* and *Shikshar Samajtattik Dristibhongi.*

A TEXTBOOK OF
COMMUNICATION SKILL

Mudassar Nazar Baidya
M.A. (Education), B.Ed.
Assistant Professor, Department of Education
Udaynarayanpur Madhabilata Mahavidyalaya,
Howrah, West Bengal.

Former Assistant Teacher,
Majhira Noorani High Madrasah (H.S.),
Murshidabad, West Bengal.

CONCEPT PUBLISHING COMPANY PVT. LTD.
NEW DELHI - 110059

© Author

All rights reserved. No part of this work may be reproduced, stored, adapted, or transmitted in any form or by any means, electronic, mechanical, photocopying, micro-filming recording or otherwise, or translated in any language, without the prior written permission of the copyright owner and the publisher. The book is sold subject to the condition that it shall not, by way of trade or otherwise, be lent, resold, hired out, or otherwise circulated without the prior publisher's written consent in any form of binding or cover other than that in which it is published.

The views and opinions expressed in this book are editor/author(s) own and the facts reported by them/her have been verified to the extent possible, and the publishers are not in any way liable for the same.

ISBN: 978-93-5594-728-4 (HB)
ISBN: 978-93-5594-844-1 (PB)

First Published 2024

Published and Printed by

Concept Since 1974

Concept Publishing Company Pvt. Ltd.
A/15-16, Commercial Block, Mohan Garden
New Delhi-110059 (India)
T: +91-11-41101460
E: publishing@conceptpub.com, *W*: www.conceptpub.com

Cataloging in Publication--Courtesy: D.K. Agencies (P) Ltd. <docinfo@dkagencies.com>

Baidya, Mudassar Nazar, author.
A textbook of communication skill / Mudassar Nazar Baidya.
pages cm
Includes bibliographical references and index.
ISBN 9789355947284 (HB)
ISBN 9789355948441 (PB)

1. Communication--Textbooks. I. Title.

LCC P90.B35 2024 | DDC 302.23 23

Syllabus

University of Calcutta

[According to the NEP-2020, 4 Yrs. & 3 Yrs. B.A., BSc. Major, Minor and MDC Course in Education]

- 4 Years BA Major—Education EDC/H/SEC/1/1(1st Semester)
- 3 Years BA MDC & Minor—Education EDC/MD/SEC (1st/2nd/3rd Semester)

Unit -1 (Introduction to Communication)

- Meaning, Nature and Types of Communication
- Principles of Communication
- Process of Communication: Sender, Encoding, Receipient, Decoding and Feedback
- Barriers of Effective Communication

Unit -2 (Listening Skills)

- Principles of Listening Skills
- Types of Listeners
- Barriers to Listening

Unit -3 (Speaking Skills)

- Verbal and Non-Verbal Communication
- Public Speaking: Extempore
- Group Discussion

Preface

In the ever-evolving landscape of education, the importance of communication skills has been universally acknowledged. It is not merely a skill; it is a life skill for the twenty-first century. Recognized and endorsed by various educational organizations, including UNESCO, it has earned its place as one of the quintessential skills for the modern era. In the grand scheme of twenty-first-century skills, effective communication stands tall, bridging gaps, and opening doors to opportunities.

As part of its commitment to academic excellence, the University of Calcutta embraced the Curriculum and Credit Framework (CCF), 2022, in line with the visionary National Education Policy (NEP) of 2020. This framework has been meticulously designed to meet the educational needs of the future, and it is with this vision that the course structure and syllabus for undergraduate students pursuing four-year honours and three-year Multidisciplinary Courses (MDC) have been crafted. At the core of this curriculum, we find the invaluable incorporation of Communication Skill.

This book, titled "A Textbook of Communication Skill", emerges as a vital resource for both dedicated educators and eager students. It has been meticulously constructed to meet the precise demands and requirements of the Communication

Skills syllabus, providing a comprehensive and accessible textbook for those who embark on this academic journey.

The contents of the book are structured around the guidelines set by the University of Calcutta, divided into three chapters, thoughtfully designed to impart the necessary knowledge and skills. Additionally, you will find questions to challenge and deepen your understanding, along with a carefully curated bibliography to further your exploration in the world of effective communication.

The realization of this book has been a collaborative effort, and I would like to extend my heartfelt gratitude to the publisher and all the individuals who have been instrumental in bringing this project to fruition. It is their dedication and hard work that has made this book a reality.

Finally, I wish to emphasize that this book is not static; it is a living resource that can only grow and improve with your input. Your criticism and suggestions, whether you are a student, an educator, or anyone interested in the art of communication, are warmly welcomed. Your feedback will guide future iterations of this work, ensuring that it remains a relevant and valuable companion on your journey to mastering the art of communication.

New Town **Mudassar Nazar Baidya**
Kolkata, 2023

Contents

Chapter
1

Introduction to Communication

1.1 Concept and Meaning of Communication

Imagine if we could not talk to each other or partake our studies —that would be really hard, right? Suppose of communication like a ground that helps us connect with people, groups, and indeed big associations. It's like having a friendly converse with someone or talking to a bunch of people to tell them what is on our minds. No matter if we are at work, in a shop, at the croaker's, or just at home, we are always participating information with different people. This sharing of studies and dispatches is what we call communication. It's commodity essential for humans and groups to survive and work together. Through speaking, writing, and indeed using gestures, we communicate our passions, share data, and exchange ideas. It's like the meter of our work and personal lives. However, simply talking is not enough. We need to communicate effectively, which means participating information in a way that gets the right response. In associations, leaders need to communicate well to guide and manage their brigades. For illustration, in academy examinations, being suitable to talk about a content helps you do well. Communication generally involves both giving and entering information from others. Once the communication is transferred, entered, and understood, the communication is complete. It's like a back-and-forth inflow of information. Flash back, communication is not only about words —it is also about how we act, write, talk, and present ourselves. People judge us grounded on how we communicate. Successful people know how to talk to get what they want without being mean. Whether it is with musketeers, guests, co-workers, or heads, having good communication chops is really important. Communication plays a huge part in how people connect with each other. When we work together in groups, we owe a lot to communication. It helped us break really big problems that we could not handle on our own. It is enough clear how important communication matters for our progress and overall well-being. In associations, good communication is absolutely necessary. Directors use effective communication to make plans, opinions, and structures work easily. It is a super important part of managing, just like planning and organizing. Without communication, effects simply do not get fulfilled. Communication keeps everyone in the circle and interested. Indeed if we write down our ideas, they come to life when we talk about them. Suppose of it as the association's nervous system—just like how our jitters make our bodies work easily. Communication gives energy and strength to the whole association. It's like the energy that keeps everything moving forward.

The word "communication" comes from a Latin word "communis", which means "common". This hints that communication is each about participating effects that numerous of us have in common, like ideas, data, opinions, and understanding. Imagine communication as a system to partake and insure that everyone understands these common effects. It's like making sure our communication really sinks in with others. Suppose of communication as a tool we use to transfer information and help others understand our studies. We do this by talking and using conduct to change information. This helps us grasp what others are trying to say, including their data, ideas, and opinions.

Communication is commodity we use for different reasons to partake, control, influence, and inspire others. At the simplest position, communication helps us control situations. Moving up a bit, communication helps us transmit information. Going further, communication lets us impact others' studies and conduct. But the most important form of communication is when we inspire others. Communication plays a pivotal part in a classroom because it helps connect the teacher with the scholars, no matter how the assignments are tutored. It is important to establish a strong connection between the teacher and the scholars so that the educational pretensions of the academy, as well as the process of literacy and tutoring, can be successfully achieved.

1.2 Definitions of Communication

To grasp the meaning of communication, let's explore a few definitions:

D. Berlo defines communication as "a process of interaction of ideas between the communicator and the receiver to arrive at a common understanding for mutual benefit".

According to **Koontz and Weinrich**, "communication is the transfer of information from a sender to a receiver, with the information being understood by the receiver".

Terry and Franklin describe communication "as the art of developing and attaining understanding between people. It is the process of exchanging information and feelings between two or more people and is essential for effective management".

Allen Louis defines communication "as the sum of all things one person does when they want to create understanding in the mind of another. It is a bridge of meaning that involves telling, listening, and understanding".

Stoner and Wankel state that "communication is the process by which people attempt to share meaning *via* the transmission of symbolic messages".

T.S. Mathews acknowledges that "Communication is something so simple and difficult that we can never put it in simple words".

In his book "**Communication in Business**", **Peter Little** offers a definition: "Communication is the process by which information is transmitted between individuals and/or organizations so that an understanding response results".

The first definition emphasizes communication as an interaction and exchange of ideas between individuals. In the second definition, the spotlight is on 'information' as the central concept; communication involves transmitting 'information.' However, this definition falls short of specifying the nature of the conveyed information. The third definition fills this gap by acknowledging that communication conveys not just concrete facts and clear-cut ideas and opinions, but also emotions.

At times, a communicator's attitude or emotional state might unintentionally accompany the information shared. For instance, high praise can be spoken with a scoffing tone, undermining the intended meaning of the words. Similarly, displays of bravery might mask an underlying sense of timidity, discernible through facial expressions.

A comprehensive definition by **William Scott**, particularly appealing to students of 'business communication', is as follows: "Managerial communication is a process that involves the transmission and accurate replication of ideas, ensured by feedback, to elicit actions that will accomplish organizational goals".

This definition highlights following points:

1. Communication involves transmitting ideas.
2. Ideas must be accurately replicated in the receiver's mind.
3. Feedback ensures accurate replication by the receiver's response, forming a two-way communication process.
4. The goal of all communication is to prompt action.

While comprehensive, two observations can be made:

1. The concept of ideas should encompass emotions.
2. The purpose of communication might not always be to elicit action; gathering information or persuading others can be equally important objectives.

1.3 Nature and Characteristics of Communication

Communication is when people partake their studies, ideas, passions, and more with each other. This sharing happens using effects like speaking, writing, or indeed using gestures. Let's talk about the nature and characteristics of communication.

1. Communication is connected to mortal exertion: Communication is nearly related to every part of mortal life. It is important in effects like having a good life, talking to others, and indeed erecting successful societies. All of these effects need communication to be.

2. Communication involves two or further parties: Whenever we communicate, there are at least two people involved. The person who gives the information is called the sender, and the person who receives the information is called the receiver. Occasionally, a sender can partake a communication with numerous receivers.

3. Communication can be one-way or two-way: Communication can work in two different ways. In two-way communication, the person who receives the communication sends back their studies to the sender. This helps both sides understand each other better. In one-way communication, information only goes from the sender to the receiver. Then, the receiver does not partake their studies back with the sender.

4. Good communication needs understanding: Communication works best when the receiver understands the communication the sender is giving. However, the sender will not know if the communication was understood. If the receiver does not partake their studies with the sender. So, for communication to be effective, both sides need to know how the other feels.

5. Communication in associations happens in different ways: In places like businesses, communication can move in different directions. It can go from the top to the bottom, from the bottom to the top, or indeed between different people on the same position.

6. Different types of communication have different styles: Every time people communicate, they use a specific way to do it. This could be talking, writing, or using their body to show how they feel. occasionally, people use a blend of different styles to communicate.

7. Dynamic process: Communication between a sender and receiver can change grounded on how they are feeling and acting. It's like a moving process that shifts in different situations.

8. Pervasive: Communication is far and wide. It happens at different situations (like heads, middle people, and workers) and in different corridor of a business (like making effects, plutocrat matters, hiring, and selling).

9. Two people: At least two people need to be there for communication to be. It could be between people in charge, people who work under them, or people at the same position. It might be within a group or with different groups.

10. Exchange: When we communicate, we are participating ideas and studies. People talk and understand each other better.

11. Means of unifying organizational conditioning: Communication brings together what is passing inside a group and what is passing outdoors. It also brings together the people and effects we need to do a job.

12. Verbal and non-verbal: Occasionally, words are not the only effects that tell us stuff. How someone looks, sounds, or moves can also give a lot of information. For illustration, a smile can say a lot without any word.

13. Thing-acquainted: Communication has a purpose. However, it will not be veritably useful, If the people transferring and getting dispatches do not know why they are talking.

14. Foundation of operation: Communication is not just for telling people what to do. It helps with planning, getting people agitated to work, and making sure effects are going as planned.

15. A means, not an end: Communication is a tool to get effects done, not the end thing itself. It helps manage tasks like planning, getting organized, chancing people for jobs, leading them, and making sure effects are going well.

16. Meaningful: Since communication helps reach pretensions, it is important that people understand and admire. However, good communication cannot be, If people do not get what others are allowing.

17. Interdisciplinary Subject: Communication involves using knowledge from different subjects like anthropology, psychology, and sociology. Using ideas from these fields helps communication work well. So, it's like a blend of different subjects and it is part of operation.

18. Purpose of communication: The main reason we communicate is to help others understand us. When we shoot a communication, we want the person to get it and reply in the right way.

19. Form of communication: Communication can be in different ways. It might be giving orders, explaining effects, participating information, or asking questions. It could be spoken or written, and it could be formal (serious) or informal (casual).

20. Compass of communication: Communication is far and wide in how people relate to each other. It is demanded in all kinds of associations and at every position of operation.

21. Communication is much further than words: Communication is not just about transferring and getting data in words. It is also about participating studies and passions. Occasionally, we communicate using signs, symbols, and conduct.

22. Communication is a thing-acquainted process: Communication has a thing. It works best when the person transferring the communication and the person getting it have the same thing in mind.

23. Interdisciplinary Knowledge: Communication gets knowledge from different fields, like studying body language, mortal geste, and stations. It's like a blend of different subjects that helps it work more.

24. Non-stop process: People keep participating ideas and opinions all the time in businesses and other groups.

This ongoing talking helps everyone understand each other and share information that is important for making opinions.

1.4 Types of Communication

Communication comes in three main types: Verbal, Non-verbal, and Written.

1. Verbal Communication: Verbal communication happens when people change information using spoken words. Whenever we talk and use our voices, that is verbal communication. It is really important in business and work. Inside a company, verbal communication includes talking one-on-one, having meetings, speaking on the phone, drooling casually, and also giving addresses or participating ideas in front of others. Imagine you are having a discussion with your stylish friend. You are not just swapping words, but you are also using your voice's tone to express excitement or concern. Your body language, like smiling or seesawing, shows that you are engaged. At academy, when a school teacher asks a question and you raise your hand to give an answer, that is verbal communication. It is not just about the words you use, but also about how you say them. During a donation in class, if you speak easily and with enthusiasm, your classmates will be more likely to pay attention and understand your points. In a job interview, your verbal communication matters a lot —speaking confidently and using a positive tone can produce a strong print on the canvasser.

2. Written Communication: Written communication means participating information using written symbols, like letters and words. Principally, when we use words that are written down, that is written communication. So, when you write commodity and give it to someone differently, or indeed when you shoot a communication in textbook form, you are using written communication. It's like using words on paper or a screen to get your communication across to others. Consider when you shoot a dispatch to your kinsman inviting them to your birthday party. By writing down the details, you are using written communication. When you have a academy design and you need to submit a report, that is also written communication. Suppose about shopping lists you write at home —they help you flash back what you need to buy. In the plant, writing a report about a design's progress or creating a detailed plan for an event are exemplifications of written communication. Indeed transferring a textbook communication to your friend to let them know you will be late is a form of written communication.

3. Non-Verbal Communication: Non-verbal communication involves effects like the expressions on our faces, how we use our voices, the movements we make with our bodies, and indeed how close or far piecemeal we stand from each other when we talk. So, it is not just about the words we use, but also about how our faces look, the way we speak, the gestures we make with our hands and body, and how we place ourselves when we are talking to someone differently. Picture this you are in a meeting and you notice your director seesawing while you partake an idea. That nod is a form of non-verbal communication, showing blessing and agreement. Also, when you are harkening to your friend's story and you give them a sympathetic look, you are using non-verbal communication to show understanding. However, you might avoid eye contact, and if you are agitated, If you are feeling shy. These conducts communicate your feelings without words. In a classroom, if a pupil yawns while the school teacher is talking, it might indicate tedium. Alternately, during a romantic regale, holding hands can express affection and closeness without demanding to say anything audibly. The world is filled with exemplifications of these communication types. When you are cheering for your favourite platoon at a sports event, clapping and shouting are non-verbal expressions of your enthusiasm. When you post a picture of your holiday on social media, you are using written communication to partake your gests. Flashback, these types of communication are like tools in a toolbox, and using the right bone at the right time helps you effectively partake your studies and passions with others. Incremental from verbal, written, and non-verbal communication, there are other ways we communicate too.

4. Electronic Communication: This happens when we shoot dispatches using electronic or digital tools. For illustration, when we use phones, computers, or other bias to talk or write, it is electronic communication. We can use it for both talking and writing. Phone calls, video exchanges, and web meetings are all forms of electronic communication. Emails and text dispatches are electronic notation.

5. Visual Communication: Sometimes, we communicate by showing goods rather of using words. This is visual communication. We use signs, cinema, and maps to partake information. For case, when we see a sign that shows the way to a place, that is visual communication. For illustration, when we plan a trip, we can use a map to see where to go, where the taverns are, and where we can cover. Signs that tell us about different places, like caffs and seminaries, also use visual communication.

6. Formal Communication: This type of communication happens within associations. When information is changed between workers and directors, or between associates of the same position, it is formal communication. This is organized and controlled by the association's structure. It helps information inflow fluently within the association. Formal communication can be both talking and writing. For case, when people have sanctioned meetings at work or shoot proper emails, that is formal communication, donations and reports are also part of it.

7. Informal Communication: This type of communication is less structured. It happens without following formal channels. It is useful for snappily sharing information, but it can also lead to rumours or gossip. As an illustration, when people chat casually about commodity at work without using sanctioned emails or meetings, that is informal communication.

8. Downward Communication: This type of communication goes from people in advanced positions to those in lower positions. It's like information flowing from a master to their workers. This information travels down the chain of command in an association. It includes goods like programmes, rules, tasks, and feedback about how well-conditioned goods are going. It helps everyone know their places and arrears predicated on the association chart.

9. Upward Communication: This is when information flows from workers at lower situations to their heads or advanced-ups. It's like workers sharing goods with their directors. Upward communication is constantly used in surroundings where workers' opinions and ideas are valued. This can include sharing problems, achievements, suggestions for improvement, and heartstrings about their jobs or the association.

10. Horizontal Communication: Horizontal communication happens between associates who are at the same position or between different departments. This kind of communication does not follow the scale but goes across it. It helps to speed up dispatches, coordinate sweats, and share information. People use it to meliorate understanding and ask for support. There are three kinds of perpendicular communication working problems within a department, coordinating between departments, and furnishing advice from staff to the departments that do the main work.

11. Diagonal Communication: This type of communication happens when people from different situations who do not report directly to each other talk to share information. It cuts obliquely across an association's structure. This can do because of connections between different corridors of the association. For illustration, a director in account might talk directly to a indigenous advertising director. This kind of communication helps keep goods effective and fast, but it is not the usual way information travels through the scale.

12. Internal Communication: This is the communication that happens within an association. It is between different directors, departments, and from heads to workers. Both upward and downward communication are part of internal communication. It's like all the talking and sharing of information that takes place within the company.

13. External Communication: This type of communication is when an association exchanges information with people and groups outside the company. As the world changes snappily, associations need to communicate with people outside, like guests, suppliers, and indeed the government. This helps to break problems and address issues that affect the company and its surroundings.

14. Intra-Personal Communication: Intra-personal communication means talking and allowing to yourself. It's like having a discussion inside your own head. For illustration, let's say you read a communication on your phone that your musketeers are going to your favourite eatery. When you see this, your mind starts working. You might flash back the times you have been to that eatery before, picturing the sights, sounds, and smells. You might suppose about whether you want to join your musketeers or not. You could start planning how to get from where you are to the eatery. Perhaps you indeed consider texting your musketeers to ask if they had like some company. All of these studies and opinions passing in your mind before you hit the "shoot" button on that textbook communication —that is you are communicating with yourself.

15. Inter-Personal Communication: Inter-personal communication is when people talk and partake studies or information with each other. This can be in different ways, like when you talk face to face, converse online, speak on the phone, or indeed write dispatches to each other. Principally, it is each about how we communicate with others using different ways like talking, texting, or meeting in person. Inter-personal communication means that when two or further people talk to each other, they calculate on each other in some way, and they produce a special connection grounded on the bigger social and artistic worlds they are part of. In simpler terms, it is about how people communicate with each other, and how their connections are shaped by the society and culture they come from.

16. Group Communication: Group communication is like taking inter-personal communication to the coming position, where further than just two people are talking and participating ideas, chops, and interests. A group is simply a bunch of people who have a participated purpose, and they work together to achieve their pretensions. In doing so, they admit each other's presence and consider themselves part of this platoon. When people form groups, it is a chance for them to gather and talk about effects they all watch about or have in common. Basically, it is about people coming together to sputter and change studies on stuff that matters to them as a group.

17. Mass Communication: Mass communication is like a big way of talking to lots of people. It involves timber, transferring, getting, and understanding dispatches that reach a whole bunch of folks using talking and writing. Think of it this way: Imagine you want to tell a story or share information with numerous people, not just one or two musketeers. You could do this through journals, the internet, social media, radio, or television. Mass communication covers everything about how you do that —from why you want to partake the communication to how you choose the stylish way to partake it with lots of people. It's like a big, wide world of ways to talk to everyone out there.

1.5 Scope of Communication

Communication is an essential aspect of mortal commerce, playing a vital part in particular, social, and professional life. Its significance cannot be exaggerated, as it fosters understanding, cooperation, and progress in colourful spheres. Now, we will explore the compass of communication, examining its elaboration from one-way communication to two-way communication, and its operation in particular life, social relations, state affairs, business, operation, artificial relations, transnational affairs, and indeed religion.

1. One-Way Communication: In the history, especially before the artificial revolution, one-way communication prevailed. This form of communication was primarily directive, with directors transmitting information to inferiors without room for feedback or opinions. Still, in the ultramodern period, one-way communication has come obsolete, as it lacks the inflexibility and effectiveness needed for moment's dynamic surroundings.

2. Two-Way Communication: Today's global business geography thrives on two-way communication. This approach encourages commerce and exchange of ideas, opinions, and feelings between agents and receivers, both overhead and over. It fosters collective trust, cooperation, understanding, and respect, thereby perfecting connections in the plant and promoting artificial peace.

3. Intra-Organisational (Internal) Communication: Modern associations correspond of colourful technical departments that need to work cohesively towards common objects. Intra-organisational communication, whether formal or informal, facilitates collaboration among these departments, promoting platoon spirit and cooperation at all situations. This communication type is frequently nominated intra-scalar, allowing directors at the same position to handle matters efficiently, reducing the need to involve elders in every decision.

4. Extra-Organisational (External) Communication: In the globalized business world, intra-organisational communication alone is inadequate. Businesses must communicate with external realities similar as banks, shareholders, guests, and government authorities. Effective external communication builds trust, enhances a company's image, and fosters goodwill among these parties, eventually contributing to the association's success.

5. Communication in Personal Life: Communication is an integral part of particular life, from the moment we wake up until we go to sleep. It forms the base of our diurnal relations, connecting us with musketeers, family, and familiarity, making it a thick part of mortal actuality.

6. Communication in Social Life: In moment's integrated society, communication plays a vital part in creating and strengthening social bonds. It enables people to connect, partake gests, and make connections, fostering a sense of belonging and community.

7. Communication in State Affairs: State affairs heavily calculate on communication for the administration of government functions and maintaining transnational relations. The advancement in communication technologies has turned the world into a global villa, making effective communication pivotal for public and transnational governance.

8. Communication in Business: In the post-modern age, business and communication are thick. Effective communication is essential for formulating business plans, programmes, and icing the smooth functioning of colourful business conditioning similar as product, distribution, and finance, eventually determining the success of a business.

9. Communication in Management: Management's effectiveness depend on effective communication with internal and external stakeholders. Communication is at the core of planning, organizing, directing, and controlling functions, icing the smooth operation of associations.

10. Communication in Industrial Relations: Good artificial relations are vital for business success, and communication plays a vital part in achieving harmonious labour-operation connections. Transparent communication reduces dubieties and conflicts, fostering a unanimous atmosphere within the association.

11. Communication in International Affairs: In this period of globalization, communication extends beyond public borders. Countries exchange information and cooperate through transnational bodies, enhancing politic relations and addressing global issues inclusively.

12. Communication in Religion: Religious communication involves the dispersion of religious doctrines and training. Prophets and religious leaders have historically used communication to convey spiritual dispatches to their followers, a practice that continues to this day.

The compass of communication is remarkably broad, encompassing nearly every hand of particular, social, public, transnational, and religious life. It is an necessary tool that facilitates understanding, cooperation, and progress across colourful disciplines, making it a abecedarian element of our actuality. In moment's connected world, effective communication is not just a skill but a necessity for individual and collaborative success.

1.6 Importance of Communication in Educational Institutions

Communication is like the foundation upon which people change ideas and understand each other. It is incredibly vital because it helps different groups of individualities unite and achieve common pretensions, indeed when they are in different areas of an association. People naturally want to connect with others and form systematized groups, so they must communicate to negotiate this. In our ever-changing world, leaders inform their staff about new technology, the structure of the institution, or any changes taking place. When communication is well-structured, it becomes easier for staff to comprehend what's passing and perform their tasks effectively. Thus, effective communication holds immense significance, serving both individualities and educational institutions. Then are some crucial points explaining why communication is of consummate significance in an educational institution.

1. Planning: Planning is like the original step in effective operation. Well-designed and communicated plans are pivotal for an institution's success. To produce effective plans, it is essential to have information about what is passing both within and outside the institution. Effective communication helps gather this information. Once plans are in place, they must be communicated to everyone involved.

2. Provocation: People tend to work more productively when they are happy and motivated. Communication helps educational leaders understand their staff's requirements, which in turn helps in keeping them motivated.

3. Job Satisfaction: When individualities partake information and understand each other, they feel more confident and perform better in their places. This eventually leads to greater job satisfaction.

4. Commitment to Goals: Leaders who communicate well and understand their staff can inspire them to be enthusiastic about the institution's pretensions. Accordingly, individualities come more married to achieving these pretensions.

5. Collaboration: Effective communication aligns all the factors of an institution. It connects the particular bourns of individualities with the institution's objects. Similar collaboration is pivotal for the overall success of the institution.

6. Conforming to Change: To thrive in a constantly changing terrain, educational leaders need to communicate with external parties, similar as government bodies or suppliers. A solid internal communication system is essential for this external commerce.

7. Positive Work Relations: When staff members are happy, it appreciatively impacts the institution. Communication helps leaders and staff members understand each other, fostering a harmonious terrain that enhances productivity.

8. Aiding Leaders: Educational leaders play multiple places, including interacting with elders, peers, and inferiors. Effective communication supports them in performing these places efficiently.

9. Leadership: Effective leaders exceed in communicating with and inspiring their followers to pursue both individual and institutional pretensions. Strong communication chops enhance their effectiveness as leaders.

10. Control: Icing that everything is running easily requires leaders to cover and address issues. They also need to give regular feedback to staff members. An effective communication system is essential for effective control and feedback.

In summary, communication is the backbone of any educational institution. It facilitates the exchange of information, motivates individualities, enhances job satisfaction, and aligns everyone towards common objects, icing the institution's growth and success.

1.7 Channels of Communication

Communication channels are like tools that workers use to talk to their directors, co-workers, and others at work. These tools help them partake information in two different ways formally and informally. It is really important for a company to have the right communication styles in place so that everyone stays connected, works well, and stays concentrated on the company's pretensions. Having a good blend of both formal and informal communication in a company is crucial to keeping everyone happy and productive. A breakdown in the communication channel can beget serious problems within an association. It disrupts the inflow of information, leaving workers in the dark about what the company wants from them and ignorant of what is passing within the company. When this happens, workers may start to questionable retired motives behind company's conduct or any change in its operations. Without effective communication, they tend to concentrate only on their own department's interests rather than the company's as a whole. This narrow view affects their decision-timber and overall productivity at work.Ultimately, these issues harm the association's overall pretensions and objects. Thus, to insure the effective operation of an association, it is pivotal for directors to effectively communicate with their workers. They need to clarify what is anticipated from each platoon member, insure that everyone understands company programmes, and keep them informed about any forthcoming changes or developments. In substance, directors must establish and maintain effective communication channels to optimize worker productivity and insure the association runs easily. This way, everyone is on the same runner, and the company can achieve its objects efficiently. There are two main types of communication channels:

1. Formal Communication Channel: Formal communication is when you follow the sanctioned rules of communication set by the company. This is important for important stuff like adverts and opinions. It helps the company run easily. It is the sanctioned way that information moves in a company. Directors control this channel in their sanctioned places. It is used for sanctioned stuff like important news, opinions, and it follows the company's structure. This channel goes up, down, and sideways through the association scale. A formal communication channel serves as a structured means of conveying pivotal information within an association, encompassing details like the association's objects, programmes, and procedures. Within this communication channel, dispatches cleave to a scale, with information forming from a director and slinging down to their inferiors, who latterly transmit it to the coming league of staff. An illustration of a formal communication channel is instanced by a company's newsletter, which effectively imparts the company's objects and overarching vision to both workers and guests. likewise, it encompasses the dispersion of information through memoranda, reports, directives, and the scheduling of meetings along the established chain of command.

2. Informal Communication Channel: Informal communication is like drooling with your co-workers during breaks or outside of work. It is not sanctioned, but it is still important because it helps people bond and share news. It's like the unofficial way people chat at work. It is about social conditions and does not watch about job titles. It happens when people with common interests or who hang out together partake news. Within a structured work terrain, an informal communication network always coexists. The rigid hierarchical communication frame alone cannot operate effectively, challenging a fresh channel outside this structure. Although this form of communication may sometimes disrupt the established chain of command, complete directors must strike a delicate balance between the formal and informal channels. An case of an informal communication channel can be observed during noontime gatherings in the association's cafeteria or canteen. In this relaxed setting, workers engage in conversations, and directors laboriously addressing hand queries with hands—on approach also illustrate informal communication. Likewise, enterprise like quality circles, cooperation endeavours, and colourful training programmes operate outside the established chain of command, falling within the realm of informal communication channels.

1.8 Principles of Communication/Effective Communication

Principles are like rules that help us do things better to reach our goals. When we talk to each other, there are some important rules to follow to make sure we understand each other. This is also true for businesses. Here are the seven important rules for good communication, called the 7C's of communication: Conciseness, Clarity, Correctness, Concreteness, Completeness, Courteousness, Coherence. The seven basic principles and other important principles of effective communication are elaborated below:

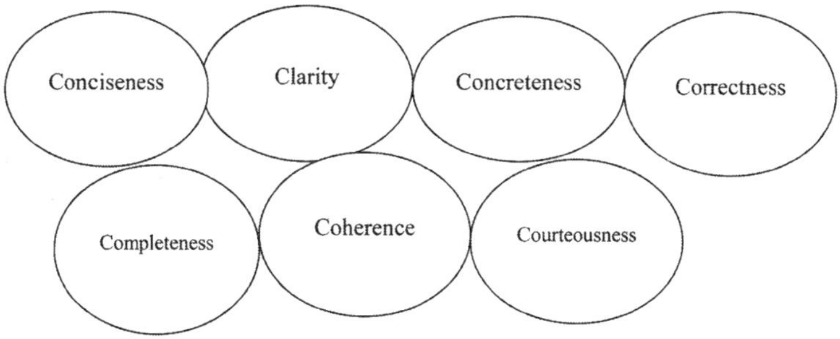

Fig. 1.1: Basic Principles of Communication

Source: Adapted by Author.

1. *Conciseness Principle*

The first principle of communication is Conciseness. Keeping your message short and clear is like giving people the most important information without any extra fluff. This saves time and money for both the sender and receiver. Imagine you are texting a friend to meet up; it is better to say, "Meet me at the park at 2 PM" instead of a long message with unnecessary details.

2. *Clarity Principle*

The second one is the principle of clarity. The Clarity Principle is crucial because it ensures that your message is crystal clear. When you communicate, you want your ideas to be easily understood without any confusion. Think of it as turning on a bright light in a dark room; your words should illuminate the meaning you intend to convey. During a presentation, clear language and a straightforward tone help the audience follow your points effortlessly.

3. *Correctness Principle*

Correctness is another important principle of communication. The correctness principle is like the grammar and spelling police. It ensures that your message is not just understandable but also accurate. Using the right language builds trust and credibility. Just like you would not want a recipe with the wrong ingredients, you want your messages to be free of errors, especially in professional communication like emails or business documents.

4. *Concreteness Principle*

The Concreteness Principle emphasizes the importance of being specific and direct in your communication. It is akin to providing someone with a detailed map with clear directions rather than offering vague hints or general guidance. Imagine you are planning a road trip, and instead of precise instructions, you receive vague suggestions like "head in that direction" or "go somewhere around there". Such vague directions would likely lead to confusion and potential missteps. Similarly, in communication, being concrete means offering definite information that leaves no room for misunderstanding.

5. *Completeness Principle*

Completeness is another one essential principle of communication. Completeness ensures that your message covers everything necessary. It's like making sure you have all the ingredients for a recipe. In your communication, you should include all the essential information and even tell the recipient what you want them to do next. For instance, when an online shopping site displays complete product information and a "buy now" button, it guides the customer smoothly through the buying process.

6. *Courteousness Principle*

The Courteousness Principle underscores the importance of being polite, respectful, and considerate in your communication. It is akin to using good manners when interacting with others, whether in personal or professional settings. Imagine you are at a social gathering, and you meet someone for the first time. You extend a warm greeting, maintain eye contact, and listen attentively when they speak. These acts of politeness and respect create a positive impression and set the tone for a pleasant conversation. Similarly, in communication, demonstrating courtesy enhances the quality of your interactions.

7. *Coherence Principle*

The Coherence Principle ensures that your message is like a well-structured story rather than a jumbled collection of words. Your communication should flow logically and consistently, like connecting the dots. If your message lacks coherence, it becomes challenging for others to understand your main message. So, maintaining logical and consistent communication is vital, whether you are explaining a concept or sharing information within an organization.

Other Important principles of Effective Communication:

8. *Attention Principle*

Imagine you are at a bustling party with friends all around. You want to chat with one specific friend, but they are engrossed in their own conversation. To talk to them, you gently tap their shoulder or call their name to get their attention. This scenario illustrates the Attention Principle in communication. Just as at a noisy party, in everyday communication, people are often preoccupied with their thoughts, emotions, or the environment. To make sure your message is heard and understood, you must first capture the recipient's interest. Their current emotional state, attitude, and level of engagement can significantly affect how much attention they give to your message. Imagine trying to discuss a serious matter with a friend who is in a cheerful mood —it might not be the right moment to have their full attention. Therefore, in effective communication, you need to consider the recipient's emotional and mental state to increase the chances of your message being noticed and comprehended.

9. *Adequacy Principle*

Think of the Adequacy Principle as preparing a recipe. Imagine you are sharing a recipe with a friend to cook a delicious meal. To ensure they can create the dish successfully, you must provide them with complete and clear instructions along with all the necessary ingredients. Similarly, in communication, the Adequacy Principle emphasizes that your message should contain all the required information and be presented in a comprehensive manner. It's like giving someone a recipe with every step and ingredient specified. If your message is improper or incomplete, it is akin to providing a recipe with missing steps or ingredients—it leads to confusion and does not fulfil its intended purpose. In business and everyday life, providing adequate and complete information ensures that the recipient can take the desired action or understand your message fully. Just as a well-detailed recipe ensures a successful meal, a thorough and complete message promotes effective communication.

10. *Consistency Principle*

The Consistency Principle can be likened to following a roadmap to reach your destination. Imagine you are driving, and you encounter road signs that give contradictory directions. In such a situation, it becomes challenging to determine the correct path to take. Similarly, in communication, if your message conflicts with your organization's plans, policies, or overall objectives, it creates confusion and chaos. Imagine receiving mixed messages from your boss and the HR department about a new company policy—it can be disorienting and counterproductive.

The Consistency Principle stresses that your message should align with the established guidelines and objectives of your organization. Just as road signs need to provide consistent directions, your communication should not contradict the overarching plans or policies. Consistency in communication ensures clarity and helps everyone involved understand the intended message without confusion or conflict. In essence, just as you would rely on consistent road signs to navigate smoothly, consistency in communication helps your audience navigate your message effectively within the context of your organization's goals and policies.

11. *Integration Principle*

Effective communication within an organization is akin to an orchestra producing beautiful music. Each instrument in an orchestra has its unique role, and when they work together harmoniously, they create a masterpiece. Similarly, within an organization, communication should serve as the conductor, promoting cooperation among employees to achieve common goals. When different parts of the organization communicate effectively, they can work together smoothly, just like different instruments in an orchestra playing in sync. For instance, the marketing department needs to communicate with the sales team to ensure they have the right product information, just as the strings in an orchestra need to coordinate with the woodwinds to maintain harmony. In essence, the Integration Principle highlights the importance of alignment and collaboration among various departments or teams in an organization. When communication serves as the conductor, orchestrating the efforts of different groups, it leads to improved efficiency, productivity, and ultimately, success.

12. *Timeliness Principle*

Timeliness in communication is comparable to catching a train at the right moment. If you miss the scheduled departure, you might either miss your destination or arrive too late. Similarly, a message designed to prompt a specific action loses its significance if it is received after the optimal time has passed. Consider an urgent project deadline: if the team receives essential instructions late, it may jeopardize the entire project. Timely communication ensures that actions are taken when needed, preventing missed opportunities, misunderstandings, and potential setbacks. This principle underscores the importance of delivering messages promptly, especially when they are time-sensitive. Just as you would not want to miss a train, in the business world, you do not want to miss critical deadlines or opportunities due to delayed communication.

13. *Informality Principle*

While formal communication is essential in organizations, the Informality Principle recognizes the value of informal communication, much like chatting with colleagues during a coffee break. Informal communication can provide insights and feedback that formal channels might overlook. Informal conversations can be like treasure troves of information. Employees often feel more comfortable sharing their thoughts, concerns, and innovative ideas in informal settings. It's like having a friendly chat with a colleague, which can lead to valuable information exchange, better understanding, and even stronger team bonds. This principle encourages organizations to create environments where both formal and informal communication can thrive. Just as you need structured meetings for official discussions, informal chats can be equally beneficial for fostering camaraderie, sharing insights, and nurturing a positive work culture.

14. *Feedback Principle*

Feedback is akin to receiving a confirmation receipt for your communication. It tells you whether your message was received and understood as intended. In oral communication, it's like seeing someone nod in agreement or ask questions for clarification. In written communication, it might take a bit longer, but it is equally crucial. Imagine sending an important email with project instructions, and you receive no response or acknowledgement. Without feedback, you are left wondering if your message got through, and this uncertainty can lead to confusion and misalignment. This principle underscores the importance of actively seeking and providing feedback in communication. Whether through verbal confirmation, written responses, or other means, feedback ensures that both parties are on the same page. Effective communication does not stop at sending a message; it includes the assurance that the message was received and understood correctly.

15. *Two-Way Communication Principle*

Think of two-way communication as a genuine conversation where both sides share their thoughts and ideas, just like having a dialogue instead of a monologue. Imagine a phone call where only one person talks while the other remains silent —it is not a productive exchange of information. Effective communication necessitates both sending and receiving messages. It is about actively listening to others' thoughts, ideas, concerns, and feedback. One-way communication, where you only send messages and do not pay attention to the responses, is not as effective as two-way communication. In organizations, two-way communication is vital for collaboration, problem-solving, and decision-making. It allows for the exchange of diverse perspectives and ensures that everyone's input is considered. Just as in a conversation, where both parties contribute to meaningful dialogue, two-way communication fosters engagement, understanding, and better outcomes.

16. *Mutual Trust Principle*

Trust in communication is like the glue that holds relationships together. It is the foundation of effective interaction. When there is mutual trust between the sender and receiver, communication flows smoothly. Trust means having confidence that your message will be received and understood as intended. Just as in personal relationships, when trust is present, there is a sense of security and openness in communication. Employees who trust their leaders are more likely to share their thoughts and concerns. Trust fosters open and productive interactions, enhancing collaboration and teamwork. Building trust in communication requires consistency, transparency, and honesty. Like a well-maintained bridge in a relationship, trust enables messages to cross smoothly, without the fear of misunderstanding or misinterpretation.

17. *Principle of Persuasiveness*

Persuasion in communication is like convincing someone to see a movie you love. It is about using credible information, emotional appeal, and logical arguments to persuade others to take a particular action, adopt a specific viewpoint, or make a decision in your favour. Just as a persuasive speaker combines ethos (credibility), pathos (emotion), and logos (logic) to sway an audience, effective communicators use these elements to craft persuasive messages. They establish their credibility, appeal to emotions, and present compelling arguments to influence others. Whether you are trying to sell a product, gain support for an idea, or motivate someone to take action, the Principle of Persuasiveness reminds us that effective communication involves the art of convincing and influencing others in a respectful and ethical manner.

18. *Good Listener Principle*

Being a good listener in communication is like being an attentive audience during a concert. Executives, supervisors, and team members alike must listen actively and patiently when others are communicating. Just as an engaged audience enhances the performance, active listening improves the quality of communication. Active listening means not only hearing the words spoken but also understanding the underlying message, considering the speaker's perspective, and asking relevant questions. Being a good listener is a fundamental skill that fosters better relationships, resolves conflicts, and leads to more effective communication overall. In organizations, leaders who are good listeners are often seen as approachable and empathetic, which encourages open and honest communication.

19. *Channel of Communication Principle*

Choosing the right channel of communication is like selecting the best mode of transportation for a journey. It involves considering factors such as speed, directness, and suitability for the message. Just as you would not take a plane for a short, local trip, you would not use an overly complex communication channel for a simple message. The Channel of Communication Principle highlights the importance of selecting an appropriate medium for your message, whether it is an email, face-to-face meeting, phone call, or a written report. Additionally, ensuring the accuracy of the message is crucial to prevent misunderstandings or misinterpretations. Just as selecting the right transportation mode saves time and resources, choosing the correct communication channel ensures that your message reaches its destination effectively, without unnecessary complications.

20. *Continuing Process Principle*

Think of communication as an ongoing conversation, not a one-time event. It should be habitual and automatic, like breathing. The goal is complete understanding, which requires constant listening, reading, and exchanging information. The Continuing Process Principle emphasizes that communication is not a static act but a dynamic and continuous one. Like the heartbeat of an organization, communication should persist, adapt, and evolve to meet changing needs and circumstances. Establishing a culture of continuous communication encourages ongoing learning, improvement, and collaboration within an organization. Just as breathing sustains life, continual communication sustains relationships, growth, and success.

21. *Communication Network Principle*

Choosing the right communication network is akin to selecting the best tool for a specific job. The network should align with your organization's needs, offer reliability, and be effective in facilitating information exchange. User-friendly communication networks encourage effective communication, just as user-friendly tools make tasks easier to accomplish. An organization should consider factors like accessibility, ease of use, and compatibility when choosing its communication network. The Communication Network Principle reminds us that the right infrastructure supports efficient and reliable communication. It's like having a well-maintained toolkit with the appropriate tools readily available for any task.

These principles collectively form the building blocks of effective communication, enabling individuals and organizations to convey messages clearly, build trust, and achieve their goals with confidence and efficiency.

1.9 Objectives of Communication

Communication is a goal oriented process. Some objectives of communication mentioned here:

1. Sharing Information: Communication is like a trace where information flows seamlessly within a group. Imagine a platoon of workers entering regular updates and instructions to keep a design on track.

2. Fostering Positivity: Think of communication as the sun that brightens up the plant. Workers admit motivational dispatches, stimulant, and recognition, which leads to increased job satisfaction and productivity.

3. Avoiding Misinformation: Communication acts as a defensive guard, filtering out false information. Picture a group converse where a dependable co-worker corrects a scuttlebutt, icing everyone has accurate information and reducing stress.

4. Preparing for Change: Communication is like a rainfall cast that warns workers about forthcoming changes. It provides them with information and guidance ahead of time, making it easier for them to acclimatize to new situations.

5. Encouraging Creativity: Imagine communication as a theatre where workers' ideas are like seeds. The further communication nurtures these ideas, the further they flourish, leading to inventions that ameliorate products and processes.

6. Building connections: Suppose of communication as the cement that binds the bricks of a wall. Effective communication fosters trust and cooperation among workers and operation, strengthening the overall structure of the association.

7. Icing Understanding: Communication acts as a translator, icing everyone speaks the same language. It ensures that information and ideas are conveyed easily, allowing all workers to understand and align with them.

8. Meeting Basic Needs: Picture communication as fulfilling the emotional requirements of workers. It recognizes their benefactions, provides a sense of belonging, and satisfies their abecedarian solicitations for tone—respect and identity within the plant.

9. Social Interaction: Communication encourages social relations among workers. Imagine a plant where associates regularly engage in friendly exchanges, creating a sense of fellowship and concinnity.

10. Aligning with objects: Suppose of communication as a compass that keeps everyone headed in the right direction. It ensures that workers not only know the association's pretensions and plans but also laboriously work towards them.

1.10 Functions of Communication

Communication has a few definite functions. These are:

1. Furnishing Information: Communication serves as an information mecca, much like a central data depository. In this script, imagine a dynamic feedback system within a company. Workers have a platform to openly partake their enterprises, ideas, and performance-related feedback. They can submit their studies through meetings, checks, or digital channels. Operation, acting as the system's responsive core, reviews this feedback regularly. They assay it to gain perceptivity into hand requirements and assess performance. It is analogous to reviewing data points that indicate hand satisfaction, work-related challenges, or areas where support is needed. Once the data is reused, operation responds by furnishing guidance, support, and results. This may involve enforcing changes in programmes, offering training programmes, or addressing specific issues raised by workers. It is akin to making adaptations grounded on data analysis to ameliorate overall system effectiveness.

2. Giving Commands and Instructions: Communication takes on the part of a captain guiding a symphony. Within an association, this means delivering clear, precise commands, and instructions to workers. Just like a symphony captain directs musicians to play specific notes at precise times, communication ensures that workers understand their places and liabilities in achieving the association's objects. Imagine a director addressing a platoon, furnishing step-by-step instructions for a new design. This communication clarifies the tasks, timelines, and pretensions. It is similar to a captain leading musicians to harmoniously play their assigned instruments, each contributing to the overall composition. Effective communication in this function ensures that workers not only comprehend their tasks but also grasp the bigger picture of how their benefactions fit into the association's pretensions. It is akin to the captain conveying the musical vision to the symphony, icing a cohesive and beautiful performance.

3. Provocation: Think of communication as a trainer inspiring a sports platoon. In the plant, communication serves as the motivational trainer. It recognizes workers' sweats and achievements, sets clear pretensions, and provides the stimulant demanded for them to perform at their stylish. Picture a director admitting a hand's hard work, praising their accomplishments, and outlining unborn targets. This communication boosts morale, fosters a sense of achievement, and motivates workers to continue outstripping. Effective motivational communication goes beyond just admitting success; it also involves addressing challenges constructively and furnishing support. It's like a trainer not only celebrating triumphs but also offering guidance to overcome obstacles and ameliorate performance.

4. Integration: Imagine communication as the cement that holds together different pieces of a mystification. In the organizational environment, this function ensures that the sweats and conditioning of workers seamlessly align with the broader objects of the company. Picture a script where colourful brigades within an association unite to launch a new product. Effective communication coordinates these brigades, icing that each unit is work fits together like pieces of a mystification. It's like assembling a mystification where each piece contributes to creating the complete and successful picture of the product launch. This function involves easing collaboration, setting clear prospects, and aligning sweats towards a common thing. It ensures that everyone understands their part in achieving the association's objects, performing in a harmonious and effective workflow.

1.11 Significance of Communication in the Organisation

Workplace communication is the transmission of information or communication between workforces in an association and an important aspect of an association. It helps associations to operate their businesses effectively. Effective communication at the plant also facilitates raising morale, productivity, and responsibility of workers. In the absence of pool communication in an association, different adverse goods can be there like high hand development, the decline in productivity, resource destruction, etc. Effective communication plays an important part in controlling these. Below are the advantages or significance of communication in the workplace:

1. Enhances Team: Effective communication at the institute helps in developing strong brigades. While communicating with each other, the staff shares their ideas and disburses their duties by uniting and this enhances the platoon spirit. Plant communication also helps in keeping workers morale high by making all platoon members inversely important in the plant. This eventually increases platoon spirit and a positive station among workers.

2. Growth Booster: Effective plant communication enhances business growth by adding plant productivity, optimum application of coffers etc.

3. Enhances Invention and Creativity: Without plant communication, workers or the pool would not be suitable to communicate or present their ideas and this hampers the creativity and growth of workers. So, effective communication at the plant among workforces encourages creative and innovative ideas.

4. Boosts Productivity: If the pool can communicate effectively and also the administrator communicates duly with the platoon also it helps in adding their work effectiveness in completing the assigned systems in lower time. This eventually helps in adding productivity.

5. Increases Effectiveness: Poor communication compromises effectiveness, as well as the overall quality of work. When instructions are not handed easily, miscalculations are bound to be. On the other hand, clear instructions exclude the need to clarify and correct any issue.

6. Boosts Fidelity: Effective and non-stop plant communication also helps in making staff pious to the association. Communication allows staff to bandy their professional and particular issues with their seniors comfortably and creates a trust factor among the pool. Therefore workers come more pious to the association.

7. Smaller Plant Conflicts: Communication in the pool helps in precluding or resolving different conflicts at the plant by barring misconstructions or differences of studies, working styles between different workers. Conflicts in plant generally arises due to mistaking. Mistaking arises if both agents have different communication patterns but they feel that the way they are communicating with each other is well enough. This may lead to conflicts. The dissatisfaction of emotional requirements occasionally people feel that their emotional requirements are not being satisfied while communicating with someone. The sense of discourteousness or casualness can induce conflicts. For illustration, disagreement between workers over a particular issue can be resolved through proper and open communication.However, it may produce hurdles in their work effectiveness and productivity, if not resolved.

8. Enhances Employee Engagement: Workers feel more engaged in their work and to each other as a platoon through effectively communicating with each other. An engaged pool is important aligned to the association's objects and also motivated towards their own pretensions or targets. Communication helps in furnishing important-engaged workers by enabling directors to more understand the conditions of workers, motivational factors to motivate them, hidden bents and chops of workers, the demand of better connectivity and relation between co-workers and superior-inferiors to produce a positive and healthy work terrain for them etc.

9. Problem Solver: Effective communication in the pool also removes different problems in the plant. People bandy in an open forum or in meetings to resolve different issues and can sort out the issues by reaching common results to problems.

10. Chops Improvement: Clear communication helps in enhancing the skill set of workers by agitating their skill needs with them.

11. Improves Customer Relationship: With effective communication, workers can manage the relationship with guests in a much better way by understanding their requirements, resolving any issue or conflicts, making them understand, presenting information to guests in a further innovative way for their fast and positive response etc.

1.12 Elements/Components of Communication

There are four common elements of communication: Message, Sender, Medium and Receiver.

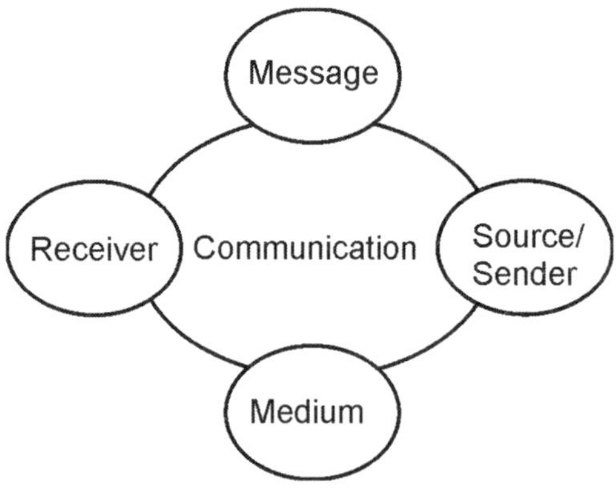

Fig. 1.2: Elements of Communication

Source: Adapted by Author.

Content or information being conveyed is referred to as communication.

Source or Sender is the individual who transmits information or communication to another person.

Medium or Channel is the system or means used to transfer information or communication between the sender and receiver.

Receiver is the person who receives and processes information sent by the sender.

The sender encodes communication using various methods such as verbal, non-verbal, or written, and transmits it to the receiver through applicable communication channels, like electronic or print media. The receiver then decodes the communication and provides feedback to the sender. For instance, speaking on the phone or having face-to-face conversations are forms of oral communication, while journals, emails, reports, and letters are used for written communication.

Furthermore, there are several elements involved in the communication process, including:

1. **Communication Context:** This can be physical, social, psychological, or temporal and encompasses factors such as location, timing, human relationships, and personal factors.
2. **Channel:** The medium through which information is conveyed, which can be visual, auditory, tactile, gustatory, or olfactory.
3. **Encoding:** The process of using symbols to express ideas or feelings.
4. **Decoding:** Understanding the received message and translating symbols into ideas or meanings.
5. **Feedback:** Providing clarity to the sender about whether the communication was successful.
6. **Noise:** Anything that disrupts or distorts the message.

1.13 Process of Communication

The communication process is a series of steps aimed at ensuring that a message sent by the sender is correctly understood by the receiver as intended. This process involves transferring information from the sender to the receiver through a designated communication channel, all while overcoming any communication obstacles that may arise.

This process follows a continuous cycle, starting with the sender sending a message and concluding when the sender receives feedback. This cycle occurs within an organization, both upwards and downwards, and is influenced by various factors. There are some distinct stages in this process that are crucial for effective communication. For instance, consider the execution of a purchase order or a telephone conversation. These are considered successful when the desired outcome is achieved, such as the supplier delivering the requested goods and the recipient of the phone call responding as expected by the caller. These elements are discussed below:

1. Sender: The sender is like the "starting point" of communication. They are the one with something to say, whether it is information, ideas, or instructions.

The sender's responsibility is not just to have a message but also to organize it in a way that makes sense to others. Imagine it's like preparing a dish—the sender is the chef who needs to arrange the ingredients (ideas) to create a tasty meal (message).

2. Message: The message is the core of communication. It is what the sender wants to get across, and it can take many forms, including spoken words, written text, or even non-verbal cues like facial expressions.

For effective communication, the message needs to be crystal clear. Think of it as writing a letter to a friend; if your words are jumbled or confusing, your friend would not understand what you are trying to say.

3. Encoding: Encoding is like turning your message into a secret code that the receiver can decipher. It is the process of selecting the right words, expressions, or symbols to convey your thoughts.

Think of encoding as using a unique language. If the sender and receiver do not speak the same language or understand the chosen code, communication can break down.

4. Transmission: Transmission is how you deliver your encoded message to the receiver. It's like choosing the right transportation method for a package.

Selecting the right channel (like speaking face-to-face, sending an email, or making a phone call) is crucial. You would not use a bicycle to deliver a package across the ocean, right?

5. Receiver: The receiver is the listener, reader, or viewer on the other end. They are the ones who will interpret the message and hopefully understand it as intended.

Effective communication means considering the receiver's perspective. You would not send a love letter written in French to someone who only understands English.

6. Decoding: Decoding is like unravelling the secret code. It is what the receiver does to understand the message. They translate the words, symbols, or gestures back into meaningful information.

-Imagine decoding as translating a foreign book into your native language. If the translator (receiver) does not know the source language well, they might misinterpret the story.

7. Noise: Noise is like static on a phone call. It is any interference that disrupts the communication process. Noise can come from external sources (like a noisy environment) or internal factors (like misunderstanding due to personal biases).

To ensure clear communication, it is essential to minimize noise as much as possible.

8. Feedback: Feedback is like the receiver's way of saying, "I got your message, and here's what I think". It is crucial for confirming that the message was received and understood correctly.

Imagine it as a ping-pong game: the sender serves the ball (message), and the receiver hits it back (feedback). This back-and-forth keeps the game (communication) going.

In summary, effective communication involves a sender with a clear message, encoded in a way the receiver can understand, sent through an appropriate channel, and followed by feedback to ensure understanding. Noise can disrupt this process, so minimizing it is vital for successful communication. The communication process can be represented as follows:

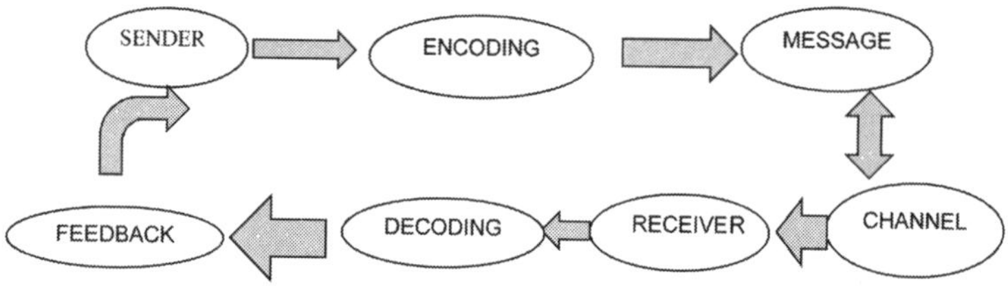

Fig. 1.3: Process of Communication

Source: Adapted by Author.

Example of Communication Process

Let's break down the communication process using an example that is easy to understand:

Imagine a Sales Training Session.

1. Sender: The sender is like the captain of the ship, in this case, the Sales Trainer. They have important information to share with their team.

2. Message: The message is what the Sales Trainer wants to teach their team. In this case, it is all about what makes a great salesperson. The trainer wants the team to learn these important qualities.

3. Encoding: Encoding is like turning the message into a language that the team can understand. So, the trainer takes these qualities and explains them using words, pictures, and maybe even examples to make it clear.

4. Channel: Think of the channel as the way the trainer communicates with the team. They might use a big screen and projector to show slides (like a Power Point presentation) or even videos with sound. This helps the team see and hear the message clearly.

5. Receiver: The receivers are like the team members who are there to learn. They are the ones who will listen and watch what the trainer is sharing.

6. Decoding: Decoding is when the team members try to understand what the trainer is saying. They listen carefully and learn about these qualities of a good salesperson. It's like learning a new recipe from a chef.

7. Feedback: After the training, the team gets a chance to share their thoughts. They might fill out a form or have a discussion with the trainer. This is their feedback, where they say what worked well and what they plan to do with this new knowledge.

So, in this example:

- The Sales Trainer (sender) shares a message about qualities of a good salesperson.
- The message is made understandable using words, pictures, and presentations (encoding).
- It is delivered through presentations and discussions (channel).
- The sales team (receivers) listens and learns.
- The team members provide feedback, letting the trainer know how they plan to use what they learned.

This feedback loop helps make sure everyone understood and can apply what they learned, and that is how the communication process works in this training session.

1.14 Models of Communication

To understand the process of communication, a few models have been discussed here.

1. Code Model of Communication (Shannon-Weaver Model): The Code Model of Communication, often referred to as the Shannon-Weaver Model, was developed by Claude Shannon and popularized by Warren Weaver in 1948. It represents a foundational concept in the field of communication theory. At its core, this model draws an analogy between communication and Morse code, a binary system of dots and dashes used to transmit messages. In this analogy, the sender plays the role of encoding information into a form that can be transmitted, similar to how Morse code represents letters and numbers.

In this model, envision the sender as someone tapping out Morse code, where dots and dashes represent specific characters or symbols. For instance, "dotdotdot/dashdashdash/dotdotdot" might correspond to the distress signal "SOS". The receiver, who understands Morse code, interprets these signals to decode the message. In the Morse code analogy, the receiver would recognize "dotdotdot/dashdashdash/dotdotdot" as "SOS".

The model posits that any disruptions or interference in the communication process occur solely within the communication channel itself. In other words, it assumes that any problems with understanding the message arise during the transmission phase. This concept of "channel noise" suggests that the medium through which the message is transmitted (e.g. radio waves, telephone lines) may introduce distortions or errors that affect the accuracy of the received message.

A significant limitation of the Code Model is its oversimplification of real-life communication dynamics. It presents communication as a linear process where the sender encodes, the channel transmits, and the receiver decodes, with minimal consideration for the complexities of human interaction. In practice, communication involves much more than mere encoding and decoding. It encompasses factors such as the sender's intentions, emotions, context, and the shared understanding between sender and receiver. These nuances are largely overlooked in the model.

To summarize, the Code Model of Communication, rooted in the analogy of Morse code, provides a simplified framework for understanding communication as a process of encoding and decoding messages. While it is valuable for conceptualizing certain aspects of communication, it falls short in capturing the richness and complexity of real-world human interactions, where context and intention play pivotal roles. As a result, it is just one of several models used to explore the multifaceted nature of communication.

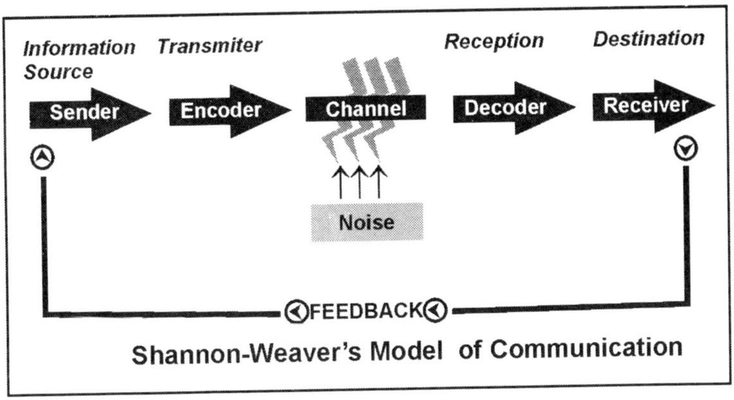

Fig. 1.4: Code Model of Communication

Source: https://www.communicationtheory.org/shannon-and-weaver-model-of-communication/

2. Inferential Model of Communication (Scott and Phillips, 2015): This communication model focuses on the idea that communication is not always straightforward or objective. It recognizes that each person's unique background, beliefs, and gests shape how they understand dispatches. Imagine it like this: When people talk to each other, they see effects from their own point of view. This means that indeed if everything seems perfect, what one person means might not be exactly what the other person hears.

In this model, suppose of the sender as the person transferring the communication. They produce the communication grounded on their studies and passions, kind of like writing a letter. Now, the receiver is the one getting that communication. They read or hear it and make sense of it using their own studies and passions. It is a bit like reading a letter —you interpret it in your own way. The crucial idea then is that indeed in the stylish circumstances, where the sender is veritably clear and the receiver is paying full attention, the communication might not be understood the same way by both people. For illustration, if someone says, "Ravi, the door is open," different people might imagine different effects. Some might suppose it means Ravi should close the door, while others might see it as an assignation to enter through the open door.

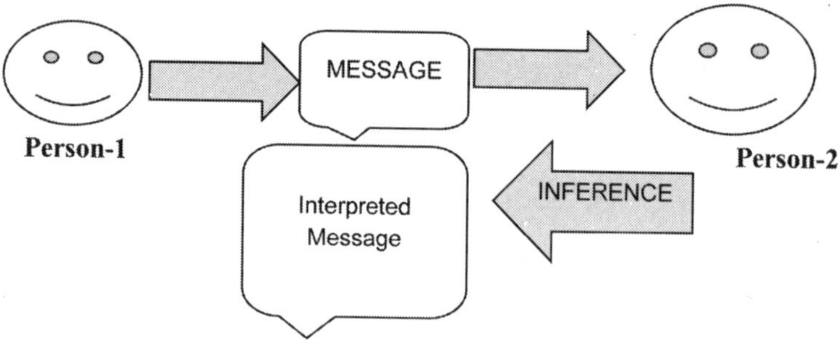

Fig. 1.5: Inferential Model of Communication

Source: Adapted by Author.

In a nutshell, the Inferential Model of Communication reminds us that communication is not like reading a simple instruction primer where everyone understands the same way. Rather, it's like having a discussion where everyone brings their own ideas and gests to the table. This can lead to different understandings of the same communication, making communication both fascinating and occasionally a bit tricky.

3. Schramm Model of Communication: In this model by Wilber Schramm, there is a special idea called the "Field of Common Experience". Think of it as a place where both the person sending a message and the person receiving it share things like knowledge, culture, language, and beliefs. Imagine this field as a place where they both stand. The more they have in common within this field, the better their communication is likely to be. The model really emphasizes how good communication happens when both the sender and receiver have a lot of things in common in their "Field of Common Experience". Think of it like two friends who understand each other really well because they have similar interests and speak the same language. Their communication flows smoothly because they share a lot of common ground. Now, Schramm also came up with a circular model of communication. It is not a straight line where the sender just sends a message, and the receiver simply gets it. Instead, it's like a circle. The sender sends a message, the receiver gets it, and then the receiver might send something back or react in some way. It is a back-and-forth process. In simple terms, the Schramm Model tells us that when people have things in common and understand each other well, communication works better. It also reminds us that communication is like a conversation, with messages going back and forth, rather than just one person talking and the other person listening. This helps us understand how people connect through communication.

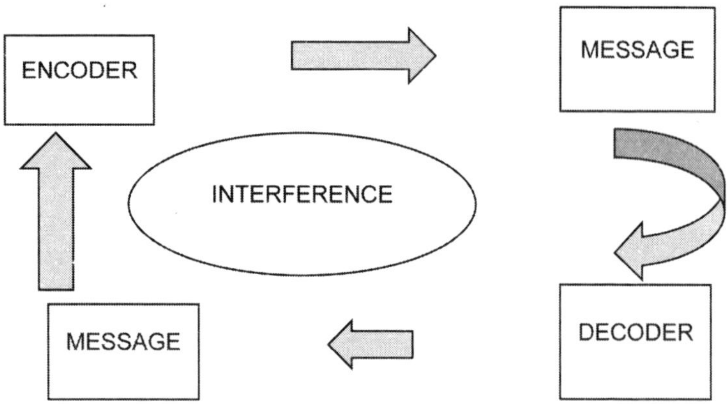

Fig. 1.6: Schramm Model of Communication

Source: Adapted by Author.

4. Lasswell Model of Communication: Lasswell's model is like a toolbox that is really helpful when we want to understand how messages spread to a lot of people at once. It's like looking at how news, advertisements, or even propaganda work.

Five Key Questions

Lasswell's model gives us five important questions to ask when we want to understand communication:

1. Who is the Sender? This is about figuring out who is sending the message. For example, it could be a news reporter, a company, or a government.

2. What is Being Said? This is all about the message itself. What's the news story, the advertisement or the idea being shared?

3. Which Channel is Used? Think of this as the way the message is sent. Is it through TV, radio, the internet, or maybe even a billboard on the street?

4. To Whom is it Sent? This is about the people who receive the message. Who's the audience? Are they young, old, educated, or interested in a particular topic?

5. With What Effect? This is really important. It asks, "What happens because of this message?" Does it change people's minds, make them buy something, or just inform them?

Understanding the Impact

Lasswell's model tells us that if we want to understand communication, we need to look at all these questions. For example, let's say there is a new car advertisement on TV.

- The Sender is the car company.
- The Message is that their car is the safest on the market.
- The Channel is the TV commercial.
- The Audience is all the people watching TV.
- The Effect is that some people might decide to buy that car because they believe it is safe.

So, this model helps us break down communication into smaller parts so we can see how it all works together. It is a bit like taking apart a puzzle to understand how all the pieces fit. In this case, it helps us see how messages are sent to lots of people and what happens because of those messages.

5. Katz-Lazarsfeld Model of Communication: In the Katz-Lazarsfeld model, there is a fascinating concept called "opinion leaders". Think of these folks as people who really know their stuff about certain topics. These opinion leaders are like the experts or "go-to" people when it comes to specific subjects. They might be the first to hear about something new or exciting. This model helps us understand how messages spread, especially through mass media like TV, radio, or the internet. So, when there is some big news or a new idea, it often reaches these opinion leaders first. They are like the early receivers of information. These opinion leaders do not keep this information to themselves. They like to share what they know with others. Because they are seen as experts or trusted sources, their opinions and ideas can have a big impact on the people around them. It is a bit like when a friend recommends a great book, and you decide to read it too. The model also points out that not everyone is equally influential. Some people have more sway or influence over others due to their knowledge, charisma, or reputation. These influential folks can shape how others think and make decisions, especially when it comes to important topics or decisions.

In a nutshell, the Katz-Lazarsfeld Model helps us see that in the world of communication, there are these special people called opinion leaders. They are like the experts who get the scoop first and then share it with others. This sharing of information by opinion leaders can really impact what the rest of us believe and do, especially when it comes to big ideas or news. So, it is not just about the message; it is also about who delivers it and how much trust they have.

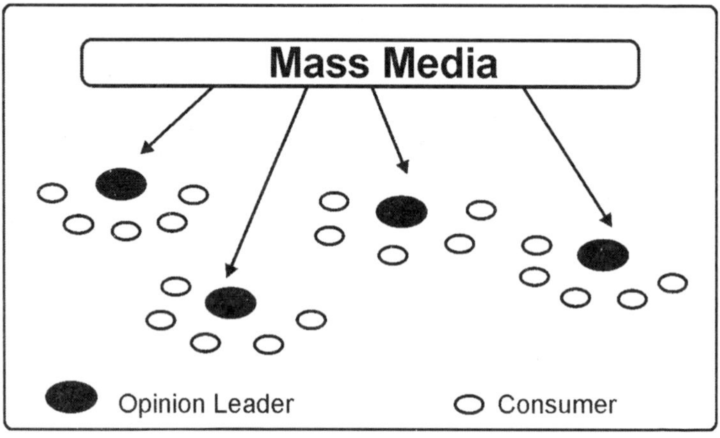

Fig. 1.7: Katz-Lazarsfeld Model of Communication

Source: https://images.app.goo.gl/ZakJU4NsAV9Lrvay6

6. Westley-MacLean Model of Communication: Imagine you and your friend sitting across from each other, having a discussion. That is the heart of the Westley-MacLean Model. This model shines a light on how people talk to each other and how it is further than just passing on information. Think of communication like a game of catch. You toss a ball (your communication) to your friend. But then is the twist when they catch it, they do not just hold onto it. They examine it, perhaps add some studies or ideas, and also throw it back to you.

In this model, communication is like a non-stop reverse-and-forth, where both you and your friend laboriously shape the communication. Now, imagine this You start with a simple communication like "Let's meet at the demesne at 3 PM". Your friend hears it, thinks about it, and also tells another friend. But when that third friend hears it, it might have changed a bit. rather of "Let's meet at the demesne at 3 PM", they might hear, "perhaps we should go to the demesne around 330 PM." This process of dispatches changing as they pass from person to person is a lot like the game "Chinese tales" or "Broken Telephone".

Then is a real-life illustration—Let's say you and your musketeers are planning a surprise birthday party. You tell one friend about it, and they tell another friend, and so on. By the time the communication reaches the birthday person, it might be a bit different, like the position or the time of the party.

So, the Westley-MacLean Model helps us see that communication is not just about talking. It is a lively exchange where everyone involved adds their studies, passions, and ideas. dispatches can change and evolve as they pass from person to person, a bit like a game where the communication can get altered along the way. It is a memorial that communication is an interactive process where we all play a part in shaping the communication.

7. Berlo's SMCR Model of Communication: Let's claw into Berlo's SMCR Model of Communication in simpler terms, give further exemplifications, and illustrate its factors. Imagine you are incinerating a cutlet. Typically, you follow a form with constituents and way. Berlo's Model is like taking your cutlet form and making it indeed more by considering all the little effects that could affect how your cutlet turns out. In this model, we look nearly at the main corridor of communication the sender (that is you), the communication (your form), the channel (how you partake the form), and the receiver (your friend who is trying to singe the same cutlet). But now, we add further details within each of these corridor, like special constituents for your cutlet. Imagine you are the sender, participating your cutlet form. Now, suppose about how good you are at explaining it (your communication chops). Are you clear and detailed, or do you leave effects out? Your station matters too. Are you agitated about participating the form, or are you just going through the movements? Your mood can affect how well your friend understands and follows the form. Your cutlet form (the communication) is now further than just a list of constituents and way. It also includes your knowledge about baking. Do you understand why each step is important? Can you explain it to your friend? Your social system and culture are like the baking traditions in your family. Perhaps you always use a certain type of flour because that is how your grandma did it. This can be part of your form too. Now, on the receiver's side, your friend is trying to singe the cutlet using your form. Their capability to crack (understand) and interpret (follow) your form matters a lot. If your friend knows how to singe and understands your form because you explained it well, they are more likely to make a succulentcake. However, it might not turn out as planned, if they are not familiar with baking or find your form confusing.

Real-Life Illustration

Think about texting a friend to meet up at a cafe. Your communication (the textbook) is simple, but numerous factors affect whether your friend understands and follows through. Are you clear and polite in your communication? Do you both know the cafe and how to get there? Social systems and culture perhaps you have a tradition of meeting at that cafe. Your friend's capability to understand and act on your communication. So, Berlo's SMCR Model helps us see that communication is like incinerating a cutlet —it is not just about the introductory constituents; it is also about the chops, stations, knowledge, traditions, and how well your friend can follow your form. It is a form for effective communication in everyday life.

8. Linear Model of Communication: Let's delve a bit deeper into this communication model introduced by Dimbleby and Burton in 1985. Imagine it as a way we use to understand how we talk and share information with one another.

1. ***Sender*:** This is the person who has something to say or share. It's like you when you have a story to tell.

2. ***Coding*:** Think of this as a special way of packaging your message. It's like putting your story in a colourful gift box or even writing it in a secret code.

3. ***Message*:** This is the actual content of what you want to say. If it is a story, it is the words and sentences in it. If it is a gift, it is what's inside the box. If it is a secret code, it is the code itself.

4. *Decoding*: Now, on the other side, the person who receives your message needs to open that gift box or figure out the secret code. They need to understand what you are trying to say.

5. *Receiver*: This is the person who gets your message and tries to make sense of it. It's like your friend who listens to your story, opens the gift box, or deciphers the secret code.

So, in this communication model, you have a sender who sends a coded message, and a receiver who decodes it to understand the actual message. It helps us understand how we share information, whether it is through words, gestures, or symbols, in a simple and structured way. You can think of it like this:

> SENDER (Sends Message) → CODING (Message is Changed, Like Putting It in a Box) → MESSAGE (The Changed Message) → DECODING (Taking the Message Out of the Box) → RECEIVER (Person Who Gets the Message).

These communication models serve as precious tools for breaking down the intricate process of communication into manageable factors. They act as roadmaps, helping us more understand the trip of information from sender to receiver. One of the remarkable aspects of these models is their rigidity to colourful surrounds. Whether it is particular exchanges, mass media dispatches, or plant relations, these models can be applied to gain perceptivity into how information flows. Communication, as these models show, is far from a simple exchange of words or dispatches. It involves a multitude of factors, from the sender's intentions to the receiver's interpretation and the channels used. Feting this complexity is the first step in perfecting our communication skill. These models also exfoliate light on the subjectivity of communication. No two individualities are exactly likewise, and each person's background, beliefs, and gests impact how they perceive and respond to dispatches. This subjectivity can lead to misconstructions. Understanding these models can be immensely practical. For case, in a business setting, knowing the Shannon-Weaver Model can help identify and alleviate communication problems within a platoon. Feting the influence of opinion leaders, as in the Katz-Lazarsfeld Model, can be precious in marketing and advertising strategies. By being apprehensive of the eventuality for deformation or misapprehension, as stressed in the Westley-MacLean Model, we can take way to clarify our dispatches and insure effective communication. Berlo's SMCR Model emphasizes the part of culture and social systems in communication. In an decreasingly globalized world, understanding these factors is pivotal for cross-cultural relations. Communication is not a one-size-fits-all skill. It is a lifelong literacy process. These models give a foundation for ongoing disquisition and enhancement in how we convey and admit dispatches.

In conclusion, these communication models serve as important tools for anatomizing the multifaceted nature of communication. While they reveal the complexity and subjectivity essential in communication processes, they also empower us with perceptivity to navigate and enhance our communication chops. Whether in particular connections, professional settings, or broader societal surrounds, understanding these models is crucial to effective and meaningful communication.

1.15 Barriers of Communication/Effective Communication

A communication barrier refers to an obstacle or impediment that hinders the successful transmission of the intended message to an individual or a group of individuals. This obstruction can disrupt the clear understanding of the message's meaning by the intended recipients. In essence, it's like a roadblock that gets in the way of effective communication, making it challenging for people to grasp the message as intended. Let's expand on each communication hedge with more detailed exemplifications.

1. Language Barrier: Imagine you are working in a global company with associates from each over the world. Some speak Spanish, others speak Mandarin, and some speak English. However, but not everyone is complete in English, misconstructions can fluently do, If an important design requires collaboration. For case, during a meeting, someone might use an English expression that does not restate well into other languages, leading to confusion.

2. Psychological Barriers: Picture a director who is feeling extremely stressed due to tight deadlines. When they communicate with their platoon, they might come across as agitated or intolerant, which can blackjack their workers and make them reluctant to ask questions or share ideas.

3. Emotional Barrier: Consider a script where a platoon member receives critical feedback on their work. However, getting protective or worried, it can be challenging for the feedback to be productive, if they reply emotionally. Their emotional response becomes a hedge to formative communication.

4. Physical Hedge: Imagine you are in a crowded coffee shop trying to have a phone discussion with a customer. The noisy background and poor phone event make it delicate to hear and convey the communication easily, affecting the effectiveness of the communication.

5. Cultural Barrier: Suppose you have a multilateral platoon with members from the U.S. and Japan. During a meeting, a Japanese platoon member curvatures as a sign of respect, but the American platoon members misinterpret this as disagreement or disinclination to share. This misapprehension arises from artistic differences and becomes a hedge to understanding.

6. Organizational Walls: In a large pot, communication frequently has to go through multiple situations of operation before reaching workers on the frontallines. However, but by the time it reaches workers, the communication is adulterated or misknew due to the layers of operation, if the CEO introduces a new strategy.

7. Behavioural Walls: Imagine a situation where a director has a character for being exorbitantly critical. When workers admit feedback from this director, they might automatically assume it is negative, indeed if it is formative. This preconceived station hinders open and effective communication.

8. Perceptual Hedge: Consider a platoon working on a design. One platoon member interprets a proposed change as an enhancement, while another sees it as a step backward. Their different comprehensions produce a hedge to reaching a agreement on how to do.

9. Physiological Hedge: Suppose about a platoon member who has difficulty hail. During meetings, they struggle to understand what is being said, causing them to miss-important information and affecting their capability to communicate effectively.

10. Technology Barrier: Suppose a company introduces a new messaging app for platoon communication. While it is meant to ameliorate effectiveness, some workers find it confusing to use. They might misinterpret dispatches, leading to misconstructions and ineffective communication. Feting these walls and chancing ways to overcome them is pivotal for effective communication. It's like navigating a maze; understanding the obstacles helps you find the right path to successful communication in colourful situations.

Apart from the above there are some specific communication barriers:

1. Lack of Planning: Effective communication rarely happens by chance. It involves careful planning, such as explaining the reasons behind a directive, selecting the right communication channel, and considering the timing. These steps greatly enhance understanding and reduce resistance to change.

2. Unclarified Assumptions: Often overlooked but crucial are the unspoken assumptions behind our messages. Failing to clarify these assumptions can lead to misunderstandings and harm relationships.

3. Semantic Distortion: Semantic distortion, whether intentional or accidental, can obstruct communication. Deliberately ambiguous language, like an advertisement saying "We sell for Less," can confuse consumers. Even seemingly simple words can evoke different responses, depending on the context.

4. Poorly Expressed Messages: No matter how clear a sender's idea is, poorly chosen words, omissions, lack of coherence, and other issues can hinder effective communication. Careful encoding of the message is essential to avoid misunderstandings.

5. Communication Barriers in the International Environment: Communicating internationally becomes even more challenging due to language, cultural, and etiquette differences. These factors require extra consideration and adaptation.

6. Loss by Transmission and Poor Retention: Messages can become distorted as they pass from one person to another, and people may not retain information well. To mitigate this, repetition and the use of multiple communication channels are often necessary.

7. Poor Listening and Premature Evaluation: Effective communication involves active listening and avoiding hasty judgements. People often rush to approve or disapprove of what's being said rather than trying to understand the speaker's perspective.

8. Impersonal Communication: Effective communication goes beyond transmitting information; it requires personal, face-to-face interactions in an environment of trust and openness.

9. Distrust, Threat, and Fear: These negative forces undermine communication. Distrust can arise from inconsistent behaviour by superiors or past experiences where reporting honest but unfavourable information led to punishment. Building trust is essential for open and honest communication.

10. Insufficient Period for Adjustment to Change: When implementing changes that significantly impact employees, it's important not to rush. People need time to adjust to new conditions for maximum efficiency.

11. Information Overload: When people receive too much information, they can respond in various ways, such as ignoring certain information, making processing errors, or delaying action. Managing the flow of information is essential.

12. Selective Perception: People tend to perceive what aligns with their expectations. In communication, this means they hear what they want to hear and may overlook relevant information.

13. Influence of Attitude: People's attitudes can predispose them to accept or reject information. When minds are made up, it is challenging to objectively listen.

14. Difference in Status and Power: When there are significant differences in status and power between the sender and receiver, it can create barriers to open communication. Information can also get distorted as it moves through organizational hierarchies.

15. Secrecy: Keeping information secret, often due to concerns about jealousy or uncertainty, can harm communication effectiveness. An atmosphere of secrecy can create barriers and hinder trust.

Addressing these communication barriers requires awareness, adaptation, and a commitment to fostering open and effective communication in various contexts.

1.16 Prevention of Communication Barriers

Let's simplify and elaborate on ways to overcome communication barriers:

1. Clear Purpose: To make communication work well, the person sending a message should first be clear about what they want to say. This means thinking about the message's purpose and how to achieve the desired result.

2. Simple Language: Effective communication happens when both the sender and receiver understand the message. Avoid using confusing technical jargon that only experts in a specific field would grasp. Instead, use everyday words that everyone can understand.

3. Involve Others: Do not plan communication alone. It is helpful to talk to others, get their input, gather facts, and choose the best way to deliver the message. For example, a manager might ask a colleague to review an important memo before sending it to the whole organization. Also, make sure the message fits the audience's knowledge and the workplace atmosphere.

4. Address Receiver's Needs: Think about what the people receiving the information need or value. Sometimes, even if a decision might seem unpopular in the short term, if it benefits them in the long run, it can be better accepted. For instance, if a company shortens the work-week, they should explain how it will help the company compete better and prevent layoffs.

5. Consider Tone and Style: How you say something matters as much as what you say. The tone of voice, the words you choose, and how well they match can affect how people react to your message. For example, a boss who tells supervisors to practice participative management in a commanding way would not be very convincing.

6. Seek Feedback: Communication is not just about sending information; it is about making sure it is understood. You cannot be sure if the message got through unless you get feedback. This can be done by asking questions, requesting replies to letters, or encouraging people to share their thoughts on the message.

7. Emotional Connection: Communication is not only about facts; it also deals with emotions. It is crucial for building relationships among superiors, subordinates, and colleagues. Communication also motivates people to work towards both company and personal goals. Additionally, it plays a role in control, where employees understand the criteria used to measure their performance.

8. Receiver's Responsibility: Effective communication is not just the sender's job; the receiver has a role too. Listening is a vital part of this. Being an active and engaged listener is important in making communication work smoothly. It involves paying attention and understanding what is being said.

9. Clear Policy and Stimulant: Management plays a vital part in fostering effective communication within an association. To achieve this, operation should easily define its programmes and laboriously promote open information sharing. When workers at all situations understand the significance of communication, it becomes more meaningful.

10. Methodical Information Participating: Management establishes a structured system for participating essential information. This system ensures that important details are conveyed following specific guidelines.

11. Proper Channels with Inflexibility: Information should generally flow through designated channels to maintain order. Still, there should also be room for inflexibility, especially during extremities when using the regular channels might beget detainments. Strict adherence to formal channels may only be necessary for routine information.

12. Shared Responsibility: Effective communication is a collaborative trouble. Everyone within the operation platoon should take responsibility for icing good communication practices. Top-position operation should periodically assess whether any walls live in the free inflow of information, and this requires active support from the loftiest species.

13. Installations and Resource Support Operation: Resource support should give the necessary tools and installations to support effective communication. Being communication coffers should be optimally employed to enhance the inflow of information.

14. Building Inter-personal Trust: Communication thrives on inter-personal connections and trust. In large associations, it is important to ground the gap in status by fostering strong connections between elders and inferiors. This can help produce an atmosphere of collective understanding and trust.

15. Clarity and Common Language: Effective communication relies on clarity. To achieve this, communication should use a language that both the sender and Receiver understand. Nebulous or confusing words should be avoided when conveying information to insure clear understanding.

By following these guidelines, individuals and organizations can work together to break down communication barriers and promote effective and clear communication.

1.17 Barriers to Effective Communication in the Classroom

Communication is really important in tutoring and literacy, and how well we communicate effects how well we learn. But occasionally, there are effects that make it harder to communicate in class. These effects can come from the school teacher, the way we talk, or indeed the stuff we use to educate. Let's break it down.

1. Language Differences: Occasionally, you might talk else from your school teacher. For illustration, you might say "wanna" rather than "want to". It's like speaking in different secret canons. Preceptors can learn your secret law to understand you better.

2. Bad Student Behaviour: Imagine someone in your class keeps interposing the school teacher by talking loudly. It's like when someone will not let you watch your favourite television show. To fix this, we need rules like "No talking out of turn" to keep effects calm.

3. School Teacher Arrogance: Think of a school teacher who thinks they know everything and will not hear to your ideas. It's like they have superpowers and you cannot say anything. preceptors should hear to you too, like a good friend would.

4. Outside Hindrance: Occasionally, people who are not in your class, like grown-ups from outdoors, try to tell your school teacher what to do. It's like someone from another city telling you how to play your games. We should let preceptors and scholars decide how to learn.

5. Lack of Coffers: Imagine your academy does not have enough books or cool effects to learn from, like a broken computer. It's like having no toys to play with. We need to find further toys (or learning stuff) or use our imagination to have fun.

6. Anxiety: Think of a time when you really wanted to say commodity in class but felt too spooked because everyone might look at you. It's like being hysterical to dance at a party. We can make effects less scary so you feel okay talking.

7. Word Choice: Have you ever used a big word and your friend did not understand? Like saying "enormous" rather than "huge". It's like speaking a different language. We should use simple words, like "big".

8. Confusing References: Imagine you and your friend both read a book, but you understood it in different ways because of your guests. It's like having different mystification pieces that do not fit. We should talk easily so everyone gets the same mystification.

9. Disinterest: If class is boring and feels like watching makeup dry, it is not delightful. It's like eating plain oatmeal everyday. We can make literacy fun with games, filmland, and cool stuff.

When we fix these effects, it's like making a super fun playground where you and your musketeers can learn and have a great time.

1.18 Overcoming Effective Communication Barriers in the Classroom

To overcome effective communication barriers in the classroom, the following actions can be taken into account:

1. Understanding Students' Language: Teachers should try to learn the language of students commonly speak. This helps because when teachers can speak a bit like students do, it makes it easier for everyone to understand. It's like speaking the same secret code. This also helps teachers become better at talking and makes students feel closer to them.

2. Interactive Questions and Answers: Asking questions and letting students answer in class is a great way to make learning fun. It's like playing a game where everyone gets to talk. This way, students become more involved in class, and that is how they learn best.

3. One-on-One Talks: Sometimes, it is nice when your teacher talks to you alone. It's like having a special conversation. When teachers talk personally with students, it makes students feel important and heard. It also makes communication very clear.

4. Customized Assignments: Teachers can ask students to share their thoughts through assignments. It's like writing a story about what you think. When teachers listen carefully to these assignments, they understand students better and know if they are teaching well.

5. Classroom Discussions: Imagine if students got to lead a discussion in class. It's like being the captain of a team. When teachers let students do this, it helps them shine and makes them confident. It is not just about learning; it is also about becoming better at talking with others.

6. Encouraging Extracurricular Activities: Sometimes, students do other fun things like sports and music at school. When teachers go watch these activities, it's like cheering for your friends. It makes students happy and builds a strong connection between teachers and students.

7. Active Listening: Teachers should listen carefully when students talk. It's like paying full attention to a good story. This helps teachers understand what students want to say, even if they do not use many words.

8. Using Technology: Teachers can use computers and apps to make learning more interesting. It's like playing educational games. This makes learning fun and helps students understand better.

In conclusion, when teachers use these strategies, it helps everyone in the classroom learn and talk better. It's like solving a puzzle to make sure everyone understands and feels good in class. Teachers can use technology and many other tricks to make sure students have a great learning experience. This way, everyone can succeed in school.

Chapter Summary

The word "communication" comes from a Latin word "communis", which means "common". This hints that communication is each about participating effects that numerous of us have in common, like ideas, data, opinions, and understanding. Communication is the exchange of ideas, passions, and more among people through various means. It is essential in all aspects of human life, from personal well-being to building successful societies. Communication involves at least two parties, the sender and receiver, and can be one-way or two-way. Understanding is crucial for effective communication, and it occurs in different directions within organizations. Different styles of communication are used, including verbal and non-verbal cues. It is a dynamic, pervasive, and interdisciplinary process that serves as a tool for achieving goals and sharing information. Communication goes beyond words, encompassing emotions and intentions. It is an ongoing process that helps people understand each other and make informed decisions in various contexts.

Communication comes in various forms, including verbal (spoken words), written (text and emails), non-verbal (expressions and body language), electronic (digital tools), visual (images and signs), formal (structured and official), informal (casual), downward (from higher-ups to lower-ranking individuals), upward (from lower-ranking employees to higher-ups), vertical (among peers or different departments), diagonal (across positions), internal (within the organization), external (with entities outside the organization), intrapersonal (self-talk), inter-personal (between individuals), group (among those with a shared purpose), and mass communication (to a large audience). Each form serves a unique purpose in conveying information and building connections.

Communication is essential across personal, social, professional, and global aspects of life, evolving from one-way to two-way exchange. Internal and external communication is vital for organizations' success. It forms the foundation of relationships in personal life, strengthens social bonds, and plays a crucial role in government, international relations, business, management, industrial relations, and religion. Effective communication is a necessity in today's interconnected world. Communication is the backbone of education. It gathers information, motivates staff, fosters collaboration, and aids leaders in their roles. It ensures everyone is aligned with common goals and supports control and feedback mechanisms. In essence, communication drives educational institutions' growth and success.

Communication at work occurs through formal and informal channels. Formal communication follows company-sanctioned rules for conveying essential information, ensuring the organization's smooth operation. It includes messages related to company goals, policies, and procedures, typically following the hierarchical structure. On the other hand, informal communication happens in a more relaxed setting, like chatting with co-workers during breaks. It fosters bonding and information sharing, often cutting across job titles. While formal channels are vital for important matters, informal communication helps build social connections within an organization. Effective leaders balance both channels to maintain a productive work environment.

Effective communication principles encompass conciseness (keeping messages brief and clear), clarity (ensuring easy understanding), correctness (using accurate language), concreteness (being specific), completeness (including all necessary information), courteousness (maintaining politeness and respect), coherence (establishing logical consistency), attention (capturing interest), adequacy (providing comprehensive details), consistency (aligning with organization guidelines), integration (promoting interdepartmental cooperation), timeliness (delivering messages promptly), informality (encouraging casual communication), feedback (seeking and providing confirmation), two-way communication (fostering dialogue), mutual trust (building trust for openness), persuasiveness (influencing ethically), good listener (active and empathetic listening), channel of communication (choosing appropriate mediums), continuing process (sustaining dynamic communication), and communication network (selecting suitable infrastructures) to facilitate clear, efficient, and meaningful interactions within individuals and organizations, enabling them to convey messages confidently and achieve their objectives.

Communication in organizations serves various crucial objectives. It involves sharing information efficiently, fostering positivity and motivation, preventing misinformation, preparing for changes, encouraging creativity, building strong connections and understanding, meeting basic emotional needs, promoting social interaction, and aligning everyone with the organization's goals. Additionally, communication functions in providing information, giving clear instructions, motivating individuals, and integrating various parts of the organization to work cohesively toward common objectives. It acts as a central information hub, delivers commands effectively, motivates like a coach, and ensures seamless coordination among different teams, similar to assembling pieces of a puzzle for successful outcomes.

Communication is vital in organizations as it enhances teamwork, boosts growth and creativity, increases productivity, improves efficiency, fosters employee engagement, resolves conflicts, enhances skills, and improves customer relations. Effective communication involves senders delivering clear messages, encoding information, choosing appropriate channels, receivers understanding and decoding messages, and providing feedback. Additionally, it considers factors like communication context, channels, encoding, decoding, feedback, and noise to ensure that the intended message is successfully transmitted and comprehended. This communication process is a continuous cycle that influences various aspects of an organization, from daily operations to problem-solving and skill development.

Various communication models offer insights into the intricacies of human interaction. The Code Model (Shannon-Weaver) simplifies communication as encoding and decoding messages, albeit overlooking human complexities. The Inferential Model highlights how personal backgrounds shape understanding. Schramm emphasizes a "Field of Common Experience" for effective communication. Lasswell's toolbox poses five questions about sender, message, channel, audience, and effect to dissect mass-communication. Katz-Lazarsfeld underscores opinion leaders' influence in disseminating information. Westley-MacLean likens communication to an interactive, evolving exchange. Berlo's SMCR Model considers sender, message, channel, and receiver, with factors like context and mood. The Linear Model (Dimbleby and Burton) breaks down communication into sender, coding, message, decoding, and receiver, simplifying the process. Each model offers unique perspectives on how we convey and interpret information.

Communication barriers are obstacles that hinder effective message transmission. They come in various forms, including language differences, emotional or psychological obstacles, cultural misunderstandings, and physical challenges like noisy environments. Specific barriers include poor planning, unclarified assumptions, ambiguous language, and selective listening. To overcome these obstacles, individuals and organizations should establish clear communication purposes, use simple language, involve others in planning, consider tone, seek feedback, and build trust while ensuring clarity and common understanding. By addressing these barriers, communication can be more effective and meaningful.

Effective communication in education is vital for learning. However, several barriers can hinder it, including language differences, disruptive student behaviour, teacher arrogance, external interference, lack of resources, anxiety, complex language, confusing references, and disinterest. To overcome these barriers, teachers can learn students' language, engage in interactive questions and answers, have one-on-one talks, assign customized tasks, encourage classroom discussions, support extracurricular activities, practice active listening, and utilize technology. These strategies create a dynamic and engaging classroom environment, fostering better communication and learning for all students.

Questions

1. Define communication.
2. Describe the nature and characteristics of communication.
3. Discuss different types of communication, providing suitable examples.
4. What are the scopes of communication?
5. Narrate the channels of communication.
6. Discuss the principles of effective communication, supported by suitable examples.
7. Explain the importance of communication in educational organizations.
8. What are the objectives of communication?
9. What are the functions of communication?
10. Explain the significance of communication in the organization.
11. Illustrate the elements/components of communication.
12. Explain the process of communication with a diagram.

13. Explain any one model of communication with a diagram.
14. Discuss barriers to effective communication.
15. Discuss barriers to effective communication in the classroom.
16. How can communication barriers be overcome?

Chapter
2

Listening Skills

2.1 Introduction

Listening is an integral part of communication as it helps in acquiring knowledge and information. We often complain that people around us do not listen properly. We appreciate and love those who actively listen to us. Listening requires patience, calmness, and tolerance. While we are generally taught to speak, unfortunately, less importance is given to listening and listening skills. In the process of growth and development, listening plays a vital role. Without listening, speaking cannot be developed. Active listening and effective listening are becoming increasingly important. Whether in a classroom, a meeting, a conference, a public gathering, or a counselling session, listening plays a pivotal role. We speak, share, and exchange our thoughts and feelings with a good listener. Wise people talk less and listen more. The more you listen, the more enlightenment you gain. This chapter explores various aspects of listening and listening skills.

2.2 Meaning and Definition of Listening

Listening means using our ears to hear sounds when people talk. We listen to understand the sounds that make up words and sentences. It's like our ears catch the sounds (like letters, stress, rhythm, and pauses), and our brain turns them into messages that make sense to us. Listening is not just about the story someone tells; it is also about how they say it, the words they use, their voice, and how they move their body. It means noticing both what they say with words and what they show with their actions. How well you listen depends on how much you notice and understand these things. Listening is when you can understand and get what someone is saying during a conversation. Listening means understanding what someone says and responding correctly. It's like paying good attention to the sounds and words people use when they talk.

The word '**Listen**' derived from the **German** word '**Hlysnan**' which means to pay attention.

Merriam Webster Dictionary: To pay attention to sound or to hear something with thoughtful attention or to be alert to catch an expected sound.

Richard Nordquist: Listening is the active process of receiving and responding to spoken (and sometimes unspoken) messages.

As per **Nunan's research in 1998**, listening encompasses skills such as discerning the intent and extent of a lecture, pinpointing the subject matter, understanding connections between different parts of the conversation, making inferences, and identifying cohesive elements.

Listen First Project defines listening as an action—the process of lending an ear to another person to take in and organize information, thereby learning from their perspective and formulating more productive communities.

Goss (1982) gave a definition of listening. According to him, listening is like a process where you understand what you hear and sort it into words or phrases to make sense of it.

So, Listening is like using your special ears to catch the sounds when people talk. Imagine those sounds are puzzle pieces, like letters, rhythm, and pauses. Your amazing brain then puts those pieces together to create a message that makes sense to you. But listening is not just about hearing words. It is also about how they say it and how they use their body. It's like watching a silent movie along with listening to words. So, you are like a detective, paying attention to everything to understand the whole picture.

2.3 Features of Listening

Listening is the process of receiving and responding to spoken and non-verbal messages to hear something thoughtful. Let's dive deeper into the world of listening using simple language.

1. **Mental Process:** Listening is like a thinking job for your brain. When you hear, your brain is busy doing three effects. It hears the sounds, understands what those sounds mean, and also makes sense of them. Imagine it's like a mystification your brain solves.
2. **Consciousness and Concentration:** To be a great listener, you need to be apprehensive and really concentrated. It's like watching your favourited movie without any distractions. When you pay close attention, you catch all the important details.
3. **Skill:** Suppose of Listening as a skill, just like learning to ride a bike or play a game. At first, you might wobble or make miscalculations, but the more you exercise, the better you get. So, if you want to be an stupendous listener, practice by talking to musketeers and family.
4. **Encouragement:** Listening is like giving a green light to a discussion. When you hear precisely, it encourages others to keep talking. It's like saying, "I am interested in what you have to say".

5. Attention: When you hear, it is not just about hearing words like music playing in the background. It is about really fastening on the words and understanding what they mean. Imagine you are reading a thrilling book, and you cannot put it down—that is how you should hear.

So, listening is like a smart brain job where you hear, understand, and make sense of what others are saying. The more you exercise this skill and give it your full attention, the better you will come at it. And flash back, being a good listener can make your exchanges with others more pleasurable and meaningful.

2.4 Listening *versus* Hearing

Hearing and listening are sometimes mixed up, but they are not the same thing. Hearing is when you pick up sounds with your ears, like when you hear a car honking. Listening, on the other hand, is like a superpower skill where you really pay attention and concentrate on what you are hearing. Let's explore the differences between hearing and listening.

Contents	Hearing	Listening
1. Meaning	Hearing is simply the act of perceiving sound by the ear.	Listening is understanding what someone says and responding correctly.
2. Nature	Hearing occurs with or without your consent.	Listening activates your brain.
3. Process	Hearing is a sensational process.	Listening is a perceptual process.
4. Form	Hearing is an ability.	Listening is a skill.
5. Type of activity	Hearing is a physiological action.	Listening is a psychological activity.
6. Active or Passive	It is a passive physical process.	It is an active mental process.

(*Contd.*)

Contents	Hearing	Listening
7. Number of Sense organs used	Only one sense organ, i.e. ear is used here.	More than one sense organs used in the listening process.
8. Level of mind	It happens in the subconscious level.	It occurs in the conscious level.
9. Mental Process involved	Attention, concentration etc. are not required.	Attention, concentration and motivation is required.
10. Identification	It is basic and simple activity.	It is three dimensional.

We can conclude the discussion by saying that listening means you actively use your brain. It's like when you really pay attention to what someone is saying. You choose to do it, like watching your favourite TV show. Hearing, on the other hand, is passive. You cannot close your ears like you can close your eyes. Sounds just go in, whether you want them to or not. It's like hearing a car honk on the street; you do not have to try to hear it, you just do. It is involuntary, like a surprise.

2.5 Importance of Listening

The importance of listening cannot be overstated. Good communication involves not only speaking but also hearing others. Yet, many forget this second part. Let's break down why listening is so crucial:

1. **Building Trust:** When you listen to someone, they feel valued and trust you. They know you care about what they are saying. But if you are only half-listening, looking at your phone, or not making eye contact, trust can erode.

2. **Reducing Misunderstandings:** Misunderstandings are common when people do not listen closely. This can lead to problems, especially in serious situations like allergies, where not listening can be life-threatening.

3. **Conflict Resolution:** Poor listening often causes conflicts. People want to be heard and respected. When you

listen, even if you do not agree, it keeps things calmer and can prevent conflicts.

4. Empathy: Listening helps you better understand others' perspectives, fostering empathy. It breaks down biases and assumptions.

5. Improving Relationships: In romantic relationships, good listening creates a safe space. In business, it enhances relationships with co-workers' and clients.

6. Deepening Friendships: Listening is not just for romance or work; it deepens friendships too. Better friendships lead to improved mental and physical health.

7. Increasing Productivity: Listening is vital at work or in school. It helps you retain information, understand requirements, and ask the right questions, saving time.

8. Learning Languages: Listening is crucial when learning a new language. It exercises your brain and is a big part of mastering a language.

9. Enhancing Leadership: Good leaders are not just great speakers; they are excellent listeners. Active listening helps understand team ideas, diverse perspectives, and prevents misunderstandings.

10. Empowerment: Good listening skills can make people feel strong and important. When you truly listen to someone's thoughts and worries, it can boost their confidence. This can lead to better teamwork, more creativity, and working together more productively.

11. Solving Problems: Listening carefully is like a superpower for solving problems. When you really understand what's going wrong, you can figure out the real reasons and fix them together. This makes work and personal relationships better and more friendly.

12. Avoiding Hypercritical Studies: Listening chops help people hear without judging others. Rather of allowing negatively about them, you concentrate on what they have to say. When you laboriously hear, you try to understand their point of view. For illustration, when you pay full attention to a leader's speech, it makes further sense.

13. Learning New Languages: When you are learning a new language, listening is just as important as speaking or reading. It might feel tiring to hear to a new language, but that is because your brain is learning how to gaspwords.However, it will make learning the new language much easier, If you hear to audiobooks or movie discourses in different languages. You will come a master in no time!

So, whether in personal life, work, or learning, listening is a skill worth honing for a happier, more successful life.

2.6 Effective/Active Listening and It's Benefits

To hear effectively means to really pay attention, be interested, ask questions, and not interrupt or judge. It's like a precious skill where you make a conscious trouble to understand everything the speaker is saying. You do this by not jumping in with commentary or questions every time there is a pause. You also let the speaker know you are listening by using nods, looking at them, and making small sounds to show you are with them. Effective or active listening, sometimes called a "soft skill," is a valuable ability that can lead to successful conversations in various settings, such as at work, with family, or in social situations.

Active Listening Example

Wondering what active listening looks like? Here's an example of a chat where different active listening tricks come into play.

Sara: I need to talk about something. I had a disagreement with my friend, and now we are not talking. I feel lost.

Mark: It is okay, Sara. I'm here to listen. Can you share more about what happened? (asking an open-ended question)

Sara: Well, we were discussing our vacation plans, and it turned into a big argument. I'm still pretty upset about it.

Mark: That sounds challenging. It seems like you are hurt because you are not talking to your friend now. (reflecting what he heard)

Sara: Yes, exactly! She just assumed I would go along with her vacation idea without considering my thoughts or schedule. It's like she did not understand my point at all.

Here are some features of effective listening:

1. Be completely there in the discussion.
2. Show you are interested by looking at the person.
3. Notice and use non-verbal suggestions.
4. Ask questions that let them talk more.
5. Say back what they have said in your own words.
6. Hear to really understand, not just to reply.
7. Do not judge or give advice right down.

Active listening is when you listen carefully to someone, trying to understand what they are saying, even if you do not agree with them. It does not mean you have to agree or fully understand them. For example, in class, you might listen to a lecture but not fully grasp the idea. This does not make you a bad listener. It just means you need a simpler explanation. You were actively listening; you just needed more clarity. Passive listening, on the other hand, is when listening is not your main focus. For instance, you might be writing or texting during a class. You can hear the words, but it does not guarantee you truly understand them.

Benefits of Effective/ Active Listening

1. Building Trust and Good Relationships: Trust is super important, and active listening helps you get it. If your team seems distant, absent, or avoids talking to you, it might be because they do not trust you. Active listening helps you rebuild trust and have better working relationships with your team.

2. Resolving Conflicts: Conflicts happen at work, but active listening can help. Sometimes, we only see things our way and do not understand others. Active listening helps us see things from different angles, understand feelings, and resolve conflicts. It also makes work more respectful.

3. Not Missing Important Information: When you listen carefully, you remember important details. This is crucial as a leader because you often need to teach others and give important messages. If you forget something, others might misunderstand, and it can affect work quality.

4. Spotting Problems Early: Active listening helps you understand what people are saying. This helps you find problems or see signs of potential problems before they get worse. It's like finding the real issue instead of just treating the symptoms.

5. Learning More: Leaders should always keep learning, and active listening helps. When you listen well, you understand more and remember it. This is great when you are planning changes for your organization or staying updated with industry trends.

6. Feeling Empowered: Active listening makes you feel powerful and confident as a leader. You understand what is good for your workplace, communicate better with everyone, and lead with confidence. It's like having a superpower!

7. Listening and Making Friends: When you meet new people, using active listening can help you build good relationships. It means things like really understanding what they are saying, asking them questions, and paying attention to their body language. People who are good at this can start and keep conversations going.

Active listening also makes others feel emotionally supported. This can be really helpful when you are talking to someone who's shy or anxious in social situations. Research says that emotional support can make them feel less stressed. It's like a friendly boost for their brain!

2.7 Process of Listening

During the listening process, students go through five stages: they first hear, then understand, remember, evaluate, and finally respond (Tyagi, 2013).

Stage 1: Hearing (Receiving)

The very first thing in listening is hearing. It's like when your ears pick up sounds from the world around you. Hearing is like a doorway to listening. You have got to hear something to start listening, but hearing alone does not mean you are really paying attention.

Imagine this: You are sitting in your room, and you can hear the raindrops tapping on your window. You are hearing the rain, but you might not be fully tuned in to it because you are busy with something else. That's hearing without listening. It is the beginning of the listening journey.

Stage 2: Understanding (Learning)

Let's dive deeper into the second stage of listening, which is like a classroom in your brain. This stage is all about grasping the meaning of what you have heard. Think of it like this:

1. Like a Puzzle: Imagine you are putting together a puzzle. Each piece is like a part of the message you have heard.

In the understanding stage, you are trying to fit these pieces together to see the big picture.

2. Movie Plot: It is a bit like watching a movie with a complex plot. As the story unfolds, you might need to pay close attention to connect the dots. Understanding the story's twists and turns is like understanding the message you are hearing.

3. Cooking Recipe: You can also think of it as following a recipe. Each ingredient in the recipe is like a piece of information you have heard. To understand the recipe and make a delicious dish, you need to know what each ingredient does and how they all come together.

So, in this stage, students use their brainpower to learn, just like piecing together a puzzle, following a movie plot, or cooking up a tasty recipe. It is all about making sense of what you have heard.

Stage 3: Remembering (Recalling)

Now, let's talk about the third part of the listening adventure: remembering. Imagine your brain as a treasure chest where you store the messages you have heard.

Here's what remembering is all about:

1. Storing Information: Think of your brain as a super storage unit. When you remember, it's like you are putting what you have heard into this special place in your mind. This way, you do not forget it.

2. Avoiding Forgetfulness: If you forget what you have heard, it's like losing a valuable clue in a detective story. Imagine you are reading a mystery book, and you forget a crucial piece of information. It might lead to confusion and misunderstanding.

3. Staying on Track: Remembering is like having a map for a journey. If you do not remember the directions, you might get lost along the way. In listening, remembering what you have heard helps you keep the conversation going smoothly.

4. Avoiding Distractions: Even a small distraction, like a buzzing fly or a loud noise, can make you forget what you have heard. It's like trying to read a book while someone's playing loud music in the background. Remembering helps you stay focused.

So, in this stage, students store what they have heard in their mental treasure chest, just like following a map, avoiding forgetfulness, and staying on track in a detective story. It keeps the conversation going and avoids confusion.

Stage 4: Evaluating (Judging)

Now, let's step into the fourth stage of listening, which is like being a judge in a talent show. In this stage, you use your brain to think carefully about the message you have heard.

Here is what evaluating means:

1. Being a Judge: Imagine you are sitting at a talent show, and different performers are on stage. You are like the judge, deciding if each act is good or not. In the same way, in this stage, you are judging the message you have heard.

2. Sorting Facts: Think of it as sorting through a box of toys. Some toys are awesome, and some are not so great. When you evaluate, you are deciding which information in the message is valuable and which parts might not be helpful.

3. Checking for Truth: It's like being a detective looking for clues. You are trying to figure out if what you have heard is true or not. Just like a detective checks the evidence, you check the information.

4. Seeing the Big Picture: Evaluating helps you see the whole picture. It's like putting together a jigsaw puzzle and making sure all the pieces fit perfectly. You are making sure the message makes sense.

So, in this stage, you are like a judge at a talent show, sorting through toys, being a detective, and completing a puzzle. You are deciding if the message is good, true, and makes sense.

Stage 5: Responding (Answering)

Now, we have reached the fifth and last stage of listening, which is all about responding or giving feedback. It's like the grand finale of the listening journey.

Here is what responding means:

1. Having Your Say: Think of it as your turn to speak up. You have been listening carefully, and now it is time to share your thoughts or feelings about what you have heard.

2. Non-Verbal Signals: Sometimes, you do not need words to respond. Things like nodding your head or making eye contact can show the speaker that you are interested and engaged in the conversation. It's like giving them a friendly thumbs-up without saying a word.

3. Keeping the Flow: Responding helps the conversation keep going smoothly. Imagine it's like a game of catch. The speaker throws the ball (the message), and you catch it (by listening). Now, it is your turn to throw it back (respond) so the game can continue.

4. Asking Questions or Commenting: When you respond, you might ask a question to learn more or make a comment to share your thoughts. It's like adding your piece to the puzzle to complete the picture.

So, in this final stage, you are like a participant in a conversation, using words or non-verbal signals to show your interest and keep the conversation flowing. It is your chance to join in and share your thoughts or ask questions.

2.8 Types of Listening

Listening can be classified into two types based on the nature of communication:

1. One-way listening and 2. Bilateral listening.

1. One-sided Listening: In this type of listening, the message reaches the receiver from the sender, but no feedback is given by the receiver. For example, we listen to audio stories on FM Radio, YouTube, and Audio Apps, or announcements at a railway platform etc.

2. Bilateral Listening: It is more comprehensive than one-way listening. Here, the sender sends a message to the receiver, and the receiver provides feedback. For example, in a live TV programme, we can ask a question to an expert, and the expert replies to the question.

Let's explore some other types of listening using a teacher-student conversation:

1. Active Listening: Imagine you are the teacher, and a student is sharing a problem. You listen carefully, paying full attention to their words and emotions. You want to understand not just what they say, but also what they might not be saying directly. It's like reading between the lines when someone shares their worries.

2. Appreciative Listening: Now, picture a student presenting their project to the class. As a teacher, you appreciate their effort and encourage them. You are not just hearing their words; you are showing that you value their hard work. It's like giving them a pat on the back for a job well done.

3. Comprehension Listening: In a classroom, students often ask questions. You, as the teacher, listen carefully to understand their questions fully. You want to make sure you grasp what they are asking so you can provide clear answers. It's like solving a puzzle by making sure all the pieces fit together.

4. Critical Listening: Sometimes, students might express their opinions, even if they disagree with your teaching methods. You listen critically, evaluating their arguments and considering different viewpoints. You aim to understand their perspective before responding. It's like being a judge in a debate, weighing the pros and cons.

5. Empathetic Listening: In a counselling session, a student opens up about personal struggles. You listen empathetically, acknowledging their emotions without getting overwhelmed. You show you care and offer support. It's like being a comforting friend when someone needs to talk.

6. Relationship Listening: In parent-teacher conferences, building a good relationship is crucial. You listen attentively to parents' concerns and ideas, aiming to maintain a positive connection. It's like having a heart-to-heart conversation to strengthen the parent-teacher partnership.

7. Sympathetic Listening: If a student is upset due to a difficult situation, you listen sympathetically. You show understanding and kindness, letting them know you share their feelings. It's like offering a warm hug when someone is feeling down.

8. Therapeutic Listening: When students struggle with learning or behaviour, you use therapeutic listening to help them understand and develop. You listen deeply, guiding them towards positive changes. It's like being a coach, helping them improve and succeed.

9. Discriminative Listening: Discriminative listening is the most basic way of listening. This type of listening starts when we are very young, even as babies. For instance, when a baby is born and hears their mother's voice, they begin to learn discriminative listening.

10. Informational Listening: Listening to information is not a passive activity; it requires concentration, thinking carefully, and taking responsibility. When we listen to information, we become better at figuring out what it means.

Think about it like this: Imagine you are at work, and your boss is giving you important instructions. You need to focus, think about what they are saying, and make sure you understand it correctly.

2.9 Types of Listeners

Listening is the act of comprehending the meaning of sounds perceived by our ears. It is a skill influenced by factors such as attention and concentration, and it comes in various forms. Let's explore different types of listeners and their characteristics:

1. Attentive Listeners: Attentive listeners are like sponges for knowledge. They immerse themselves in what they hear with deep concentration. For example, in a classroom setting, a student who actively engages in the lecture, takes detailed notes, and asks questions to clarify concepts is an attentive listener. They are invaluable in acquiring knowledge and education because they absorb information effectively. Attentive listening is also helpful for long-term memorization; the more attention they pay, the better they retain the learning materials.

2. Inattentive Listeners: Inattentive listeners, on the other hand, listen mechanically and lack focus on the speaker.

Imagine someone attending a long, monotonous presentation but constantly checking their phone or daydreaming. Such listeners struggle to retain the material presented because they do not fully engage with it. They often forget what they heard shortly after the presentation. In educational settings, this type of listener is less desirable.

3. Imperative Listeners: Imperative listeners listen not out of interest but because they are compelled to do so. An example might be a student who listens to a teacher's instructions only to avoid punishment or detention. This type of listening is not engaging and does not foster a genuine interest in the subject matter. As a result, the retention of information is usually short-lived. Imperative listening can be seen as a necessary but unexciting form of listening.

4. Spontaneous Listeners: Spontaneous listeners are individuals who willingly and eagerly tune into a speaker. They have a natural interest and motivation to hear what is being said. Think of a person attending a captivating TED Talk or a passionate teacher delivering an inspiring lecture. These listeners not only remember the information but often internalize it, making it part of their knowledge repertoire. Spontaneous interest fuels effective learning and memorization.

5. Direct Listeners: Direct listeners are those who receive information directly from the primary source or speaker. For instance, a scientist conducting interviews or surveys to gather data directly from participants is engaged in direct listening. This type of listening is crucial for obtaining first-hand information, especially in research and academic pursuits, where the authenticity and accuracy of the information are paramount.

6. Indirect Listeners: Indirect listeners, in contrast, obtain information from secondary sources or individuals other than the primary speaker. Think of a person learning about a historical event through books, documentaries, or conversations with experts. The significance and reliability of the information in this case depend on the ability and honesty of those conveying it to the listener. Indirect listening is common in everyday life when we learn from various sources and perspectives.

In summary, effective listening encompasses a spectrum of styles, from attentive and spontaneous listening, which enhance learning and understanding, to inattentive and imperative listening, which may hinder these processes. The choice of listening style often depends on the context and the individual's level of interest and engagement.

2.10 Traits of a Good Listener

A good listener is someone who pays full attention when another person talks and thinks precisely about what they are saying. Good listening is not just about hearing words; it is about truly understanding and responding in a helpful way. A good listener might ask questions, give suggestions, or share laboriously when it is demanded. How you hear is just as important as whether you hear at all.

Let's imagine a situation: You are talking to your friend Sarah, and she is telling you about her new job. However, you will concentrate completely on what she is saying if you are a good listener. You will not be allowing thoughts about your own day or what you will eat later. Rather, you will be really engaged in her story, showing that you care about her experience. As Sarah discusses her new responsibilities and challenges at work, you will pay close attention to the details. You might ask questions like, "What kind of systems are you working on?" or "How do you handle those tough tasks?" These questions show that you are not just hearing her words but also trying to understand her situation better. Likewise, you might offer suggestions or support if she mentions a problem she is dealing with. For illustration, if she says, "I struggle to manage my time", you could suggest, "Maybe you could try using a time management app or making a to-do list. That might be helpful". Being a good listener means you are not just unresisting; you are laboriously sharing in the discussion by showing interest, understanding, and offering backing when demanded. This kind of listening helps make stronger connections with others and makes them feel valued.

Good listeners possess a unique power that shines in their interactions. It envelops them and creates an aura of trust and warmth. Conversations with them flow naturally, leaving you feeling refreshed and truly understood. Perhaps you have someone like this in your circle of friends, or maybe it is you! Here are some key traits of a good listener.

1. You are Present in the Moment: Often, we are not fully engaged when listening. While someone is talking, we are already forming conclusions and planning our responses. Good listening requires you to silence your inner dialogue and give your undivided attention to the speaker. Imagine shining a spotlight on them —all your focus is on their words.

2. Do not Distract You: Listening may seem simple, but it is not always easy. Sometimes, we are tempted to multi-task while listening. A good listener knows that avoiding distractions is vital. They put away their phone, close their laptop, and turn off the TV. This is not the time to showcase multi-tasking skills.

3. You are Curious: Interest is crucial in listening, even when it concerns those close to you. Sometimes, we assume we know everything about someone, leading us to overlook new aspects in their words. A good listener plays the role of a detective, gathering information and seeking to understand the emotions and motivations behind the speaker's words.

4. You are Sincere and Open-Minded: Quick judgements can hinder effective listening. A rash opinion can kill a conversation. Good listeners postpone judgments until the end of a conversation to better understand their counterpart's feelings and perspective.

5. Your Senses Are Attuned: Non-verbal cues, such as body language, are essential elements of communication. Good listeners pay attention to these cues and actively engage through eye contact, nods, and facing the speaker.

6. You Ask the Right Questions: Listening is not passive; it involves appropriate responses. Paraphrasing and clarifying what the speaker is saying become tools in a good listener's arsenal. This ensures a common understanding and prevents miscommunication.

7. You Accept Different Opinions: In debates or discussions, good listeners value picking up different ideas. They maintain curiosity and attentiveness, recognizing that diverse perspectives can offer valuable insights.

8. You Do not Interrupt: Impatience to hear someone's thoughts can be strong, but good listeners exercise patience. They understand that finding the right words takes time and avoid interrupting. Listening is not a race; it is about giving time and space.

9. You Stay Authentic: In situations where someone dominates a conversation, good listeners know it is acceptable to interject. They do not force themselves to endure one-sided conversations, understanding that genuine interest requires space for their own thoughts and feelings.

10. You Recognize Your Limits: A good listener acknowledges when their capacity to help has reached its limit.

They are aware that continuing to listen may be exhausting for them and unhelpful for the speaker. In such cases, they may recommend seeking professional assistance for more complex issues. Recognizing when to seek help is an important aspect of being a good listener.

Moreover, a good listener does not rush to make judgements or assumptions. They wait patiently for the speaker to share all the details and ask questions to understand better. They do not make conclusions until everything is clear.

2.11 Importance of Listening in the Classroom

Teachers are often face trouble to manage their classes due to lack of listening abilities of learners. Sometimes, teachers found students listening inactively. Lack of active and effective listening spoils all the positive energy of teachers. In this connection, points regarding the importance of listening in the classroom have been discussed here.

1. A classroom without Noise: A classroom without noise is very important for creating an excellent learning environment. When students listen to their teachers in the classroom, it becomes quiet and peaceful.

2.Benefits for the Mind: Listening involves paying attention, focusing, understanding, and using our senses. It has positive effects on our mental processes. Developing good listening habits can increase our interest in learning.

3. Self-assurance: Improving your listening skills can boost your self-confidence, which is the belief that you can do well in class. So, as students get better at listening, they start feeling more self-assured, relaxed, and ready to do well in school.

4. Socio-emotional Development: Active listening has a positive impact on social-emotional development. It encourages thoughtful thinking, leading to a decrease in anxiety and depression among students.

5. Academic Success Through Effective Listening: Students who excel in listening are more likely to thrive academically. This is because they effectively absorb information during lectures and discussions, paying attention to details instead of drifting into daydreams or getting distracted by external factors.

6. Spending More Time on Tasks: Students who listen attentively in class can start their assignments quickly without asking many questions. When a student does not listen well, they might make avoidable mistakes, leading to extra work. These mistakes might even extend to homework, making them spend more time on it. Students understand how listening affects time management.

7. Improved Learning: Listening students grasp the teacher's content better and understand the main ideas. Their focus helps them remember information, making it easier to recall and build on previous knowledge, especially in subjects like math, which builds on earlier skills. Good listeners can connect to new ideas and concepts more effectively.

8. Better Relationships: Whether students are in a teacher's class or listening to a guest speaker, showing attentiveness earns respect and trust. When students pay attention, speakers feel valued and are more open to their input. Teachers appreciate students who actively listen, and peers also respect those who pay attention to their comments and questions.

9. Enhanced Listening Skills: Teachers use various activities to teach listening skills, including rhythm games with younger students. They may say phrases like "All eyes on me" to get students' attention. Students learn that eye contact is essential for listening. By following these prompts, students develop strong listening skills that benefit them in various aspects of life.

10. Enhancing Mental Well-being Through Active Listening: When students make active listening a habit, they often find themselves thinking more thoughtfully about what they hear. This can have the positive effects of reducing stress and lifting their spirits.

2.12 Barriers to Listening

A study by the University of Minnesota found that people tend to remember only about half of what they hear immediately after listening to someone. This fact is quite concerning, especially in the business world, where effective communication is crucial for success and growth. If you think your listening skills need improvement or if your business is suffering due to poor listening, understanding the common barriers to effective listening can help you make the necessary changes to enhance communication. Several obstacles can hinder effective listening, including physical, environmental, psychological, emotional, and cultural factors.

I. *Physical and Environmental Barriers*

Effective listening faces various challenges, with physical obstacles being the most apparent. These obstacles can include factors that physically hinder one's ability to hear what's being said. It could be a significant distance between speakers, excessive external noise, or physical barriers blocking sound transmission. Moreover, environmental conditions like temperature and lighting can also impact listening. An uncomfortably hot room, for instance, might divert attention from the speaker, while a dimly lit space could lead to fatigue and reduced engagement. Even the arrangement of furniture can influence listening. Some seating configurations promote attentive listening, while others discourage it and create physical barriers that separate individuals. Understanding and addressing these physical and environmental factors can greatly enhance the quality of communication.

1. Too Much Noise: When there is a lot of background noise, it is tough to listen effectively. This can happen at a noisy party, in a crowded room, or even when the TV is on in the background.

2. Juggling Multiple Conversations: Trying to listen to more than one conversation at once can be tricky. This might occur when the TV or radio is playing while you are talking to someone, or when you are on the phone with one person while chatting with another in the same room. It's like trying to split your attention.

3. Distractions Around You: Our brains can easily get side-tracked. A passing movement outside the window or a random thought can disrupt your listening. Even smartphone notifications can be a big distraction. That's why it is a good idea to put your phone away when someone wants to talk. Some people doodle or fiddle with things to stay focused, but for others, it is just a way to keep their hands busy without losing focus.

4. Focus on Attractiveness or Accent: Sometimes, you might pay more attention to how attractive or unattractive someone is, or you get caught up in their accent rather than what they are saying. It's like listening to the melody but missing the lyrics.

5. Lack of Interest: When you are not interested in the topic being discussed, boredom creeps in quickly. This boredom can lead to distraction and a loss of attention.

6. Physical Discomfort: Feeling unwell, tired, hungry, thirsty, too hot, too cold, or needing to use the restroom can be major distractions. It is almost impossible to concentrate when you are physically uncomfortable.

7. External Stress: When you are stressed about other things happening in your life, it is hard to quiet your inner thoughts and focus on someone else.

8. Phone *versus* Face-to-Face: Communicating over the phone is different from speaking face-to-face because you miss out on body language and facial expressions. This means you have to concentrate more on the conversation. Using tone of voice effectively can help get your message across clearly.

9. Language and Understanding: If you do not quite understand what someone is saying due to their choice of words or a strong accent, it is tempting to tune out. Instead, try to listen more attentively and do not hesitate to ask for clarification if needed.

II. *Cultural Barriers*

When individuals come from diverse backgrounds, be it in terms of religion, ethnicity, culture, or other factors, it can lead to cultural barriers that hinder effective listening. These barriers arise because people from different cultures may have distinct communication styles, norms, and expectations. These barriers may arise from variations in ethnicity, religion, customs, or social standing. In the business world, cultural barriers emerge when there are differences in how business is conducted across various regions of the world. These differences can be attributed to distinct laws, practices, or societal expectations.

For instance, imagine you are working with a colleague from a culture where direct eye contact is considered rude. If you come from a culture where strong eye contact is a sign of attentiveness, you might misinterpret your colleague's behaviour as disinterest or disrespect. This difference in cultural norms can create misunderstandings and impact your ability to listen effectively.

Moreover, language barriers can also be part of cultural differences. If someone speaks English as a second language and you primarily communicate in English, there might be challenges in comprehending nuances and idiomatic expressions, which can hinder effective listening. To overcome cultural barriers to listening, it is crucial to approach conversations with an open mind and a willingness to learn about and respect different cultural practices. This can lead to better cross-cultural understanding and more effective communication.

III. *Emotional and Psychological Barriers*

While external noise can certainly disrupt listening, there is another form of interference known as psychological noise. This is the mental distraction that arises from our emotions and mood. When our emotions are running high, whether in a positive or negative direction, it can be challenging to receive and process information effectively. Anxiety, impatience, and undesirable listener behaviour can hinder effective listening. Psychological barriers are like mental obstacles. They happen when we start guessing what someone will say, plan our own response, or judge the person talking to us.

For instance, if you are chatting with someone and start thinking about what to say back, it makes it harder to listen to them. You will be more concerned about your reply, which can lead to confusion and not-so-great communication.

Imagine you are trying to listen to a colleague's presentation, but you are feeling extremely excited about a personal achievement. In this state of heightened emotion, it may be tough to concentrate on what your colleague is saying, and your listening ability might be compromised. To overcome emotional and psychological barriers to listening, it is important to acknowledge and manage your emotions. This can involve techniques like taking deep breaths or briefly stepping away to regain focus. By doing so, you can enhance your ability to listen effectively, regardless of your emotional state.

IV. *Time Pressure*

The sensation of being under time constraints can undermine one's ability to listen effectively. Whether this pressure originates internally or externally, it often leads to reduced attentiveness during conversations.

V. *Rapid Speech Pace*

When someone speaks at an accelerated pace, comprehension can become a formidable task. Fast speech may overwhelm the listener, resulting in an inability to fully grasp the message being conveyed.

VI. *Impact of Tone*

The tone of voice plays a significant role in communication. A monotonous tone can make it difficult to maintain focus, while an angry or loud tone may provoke emotional responses instead of constructive listening.

VII. *Interruptions*

Interruptions, whether manifested physically or verbally, disrupt the natural flow of conversation. Instances of simultaneous talking or frequent overlaps can cause messages to be lost in the chaos, leading to ineffective communication.

VIII. *Overwhelmed by Information*

Excessive information can overwhelm individuals, making it difficult to concentrate on specific details. This often occurs in settings like business meetings or conversations where an abundance of information creates distractions, hindering effective listening.

IX. *Influence of Bias*

Preconceived biases or assumptions based on factors such as appearance, gender, race, or other personal attributes can cloud our perception. Such biases may lead to the expectation of certain behaviours from others, obstructing impartial and open-minded listening.

X. *Gender Differences*

Studies show that gender can affect how people listen. Research reveals that men and women often listen in different ways and for different reasons. Women tend to focus on the emotions behind the speaker's words, while men often concentrate on facts and content.

XI. *Lack of Training*

Listening is not something we are born with; it is a skill that is developed through practice and training. A significant barrier is the absence of proper training in listening skills. Without this training, people may avoid listening to information they find difficult, boring, or complex. They might selectively tune in only to what they consider interesting.

XII. *Poor Listening Habits*

Many people have developed subpar listening habits that are hard to break, acting as barriers to effective listening. For instance, some individuals pretend to pay attention or act like attentive listeners to impress the speaker. Others might get caught up in minor details and miss the main point. Additionally, judging the speaker based on their mannerisms, voice, appearance, or accent can hinder effective listening.

XIII. *Interruption*

Interrupting in conversations is common but not always seen as bad listening. Interruptions can be unintentional when we misread cues or offer supportive or enthusiastic comments. Interruptions can also be necessary when providing directions, instructions, or warnings. However, unintentional interruptions can still be considered bad listening if they result from not paying full attention. These interruptions can create negative impressions. Interruptions can also be used to dominate a conversation, leading to competition for speaking time and potential withdrawal from the conversation.

XIV. *Pseudo-listening*

Pseudo-listening is when someone pretends to listen but is not actually paying attention. It involves acting like you are engaged in the conversation when you are not. While it can be used as a politeness strategy, it is considered a form of bad listening because the person would not remember what was said or respond appropriately. Although we all do it occasionally, it is best to avoid pseudo-listening and not make it a habit to maintain positive relationships.

XV. *Cognitive and Personal Barriers*

There are cognitive and personal barriers that can affect our listening. These barriers include limits in our ability to process information, not preparing ourselves to listen, dealing with complex or unclear messages, and having biases. Sometimes, we engage in multitasking or daydreaming while listening, which means our attention is divided among different things. Imagine your mind as having ten televisions, and sometimes, five of them are focused on one message. This can be useful or distracting, depending on the situation. To become better listeners, we need to understand how our cognitive abilities and personal preferences impact our listening and be aware of potential barriers.

In summary, active listening stands as a vital skill demanding our complete focus, empathy, and a receptive attitude. Surmounting these obstacles to active listening necessitates recognizing our prejudices, removing distractions, and proactively striving to connect with the speaker. Through these efforts, we can forge more robust relationships, gain deeper insights into others' viewpoints, and ultimately enhance our effectiveness as communicators.

2.13 Remedies for Overcoming Listening Barriers

By applying the strategies outlined below, you can improve your listening skills and become a more effective communicator in a wide range of situations. These techniques will help you actively engage with others and understand their perspectives more deeply.

1. Minimize External Distractions: To become a better listener, it is essential to minimize external distractions. Identify the sources of distraction and consciously keep them out of your mind. For example, if you are in a meeting, put away your phone or turn off notifications to maintain focus. Imagine you are in a crucial business meeting, and your phone keeps buzzing with text messages. By silencing your phone and placing it out of sight, you can give your full attention to the speaker and the discussion at hand.

Strategies to Overcome External Noise

When confronted with external noise while listening to a speaker, there are various effective approaches to improve the situation:

(i) **Relocate to a Quieter Space:** If possible, consider moving the conversation to a quieter environment. This could involve finding a less noisy room, closing windows, or taking other measures to eliminate the noise source.

(ii) **Adjust Speaker's Volume:** Sometimes, it may not be feasible to change locations. In such cases, the listener can kindly request the speaker to raise their voice, ensuring better clarity.

(iii) **Enhance Active Listening Skills:** With practice, individuals can develop their active listening skills. This allows them to filter out external distractions and concentrate solely on the speaker's message, even in noisy surroundings.

2. Prioritize Listening Over Speaking: Remind yourself that, in this scenario, your role is that of the listener, not the speaker. The person speaking is the guide, and your primary focus should be on listening attentively. For instance, in a classroom setting, the teacher is delivering a lecture. Instead of thinking about what questions you will ask or what points you want to make, concentrate on absorbing the teacher's knowledge and insights.

3. Asking Questions: There might be times when you start feeling a bit bored after listening to a lengthy speech for, let's say, three hours. In such situations, do not hesitate to ask questions. It is a great way to stay engaged and show your interest in the topic. When you ask questions, it not only helps you refocus on the subject but also allows the speaker to clarify any points. This interaction can significantly enhance the overall presentation. So, make it a habit to ask questions when appropriate.

4. Listen Carefully Before Offering Advice: If you intend to provide advice to the speaker, it is essential to listen carefully first. However, avoid rushing to give advice too frequently during the conversation. Frequent interruptions can disrupt the flow of the discussion. Take your time to absorb the speaker's message fully before offering your input.

5. Practice Reflecting Instead of Redirecting: To demonstrate your genuine interest in the speaker, practice reflecting their thoughts and feelings rather than deflecting or diverting the conversation. Showing that you are actively listening and acknowledging their perspective can strengthen your relationship with the speaker. When there is a strong bond between you and your conversation partner, it naturally encourages more meaningful interactions. So, work on practicing this skill in your conversations.

6. Dealing with Information Overload: Information overload happens when you are bombarded with too much data, making it challenging to grasp the main message. To tackle this issue, here are some effective strategies:

(i) **Request a Slower Pace:** If you find yourself overwhelmed by the speed of information delivery, politely ask the speaker to slow down. This gives you more time to absorb and process the content.

(ii) **Ask for Clarification:** Do not hesitate to seek clarification if you miss something. Kindly request the speaker to repeat any crucial point that you did not catch.

(iii) **Take Notes:** During the conversation, jot down essential information and key points. This allows you to review and organize the material later, preventing information overload.

7. **Avoiding Over-Agreeing:** Sometimes, we tend to over-agree with a speaker merely to wrap up the conversation quickly. However, this can lead to not truly absorbing the content. To address this habit, consider these steps:

(i) **Stay Engaged:** Remind yourself of the purpose of the conversation and why you are investing your time in it. Avoid rushing the discussion; see it through to gain a deeper understanding.

(ii) **Active Listening:** Instead of mindlessly nodding or saying "uh-huh", actively listen to the speaker. Engage with their message, ask questions, and provide meaningful responses. This way, you will derive more value from every conversation.

8. **Combatting Faking Attention:** To break free from the habit of pretending to listen, adopt these remedies:

(i) **Clear Your Mental Slate:** Prior to engaging in any conversation, take a moment to clear your mind. Assume that the other person possesses valuable information you do not yet have. This mind-set encourages active listening.

(ii) **Resist Formulating Replies:** Avoid the common trap of constructing responses while someone else is speaking. This divided attention turns you into a waiting speaker rather than an attentive listener.

(iii) **Take Notes:** When someone is sharing important points, consider taking notes. This helps you focus on key information and enables you to respond thoughtfully.

9. Overcoming Emotional Hurdles: To surmount emotional barriers, the key is maintaining composure in any circumstance. Prior to reacting to someone's words, pause and let go of any negative emotion their sentiments may have triggered. Alternatively, if you find yourself too upset to listen effectively, it might be best to step away from the conversation temporarily. In essence, exercising self-control stands as the most effective strategy for addressing emotional barriers.

Conclusion: Communication relies on both speaking and listening, with the listener being equally important. Therefore, prioritize attentive and careful listening. Techniques like meditating on what the speaker says can ensure that the conversation stays on track and both parties understand each other. Asking questions and seeking clarification is crucial for active listening. Maintain focus on one conversation at a time, avoid distractions, and refrain from guessing or multitasking. Active listening involves showing interest and engaging with the speaker through questions and participation. Proper timing and context are also vital for effective communication.

2.14 Concept of Listening Skills

Focusing on listening can be quite challenging, and studies indicate that people typically retain only 25 to 50 per cent of what they hear. However, honing your listening abilities has the potential to boost your productivity and increase your ability to sway or persuade others. Listening skills are like tools that help you grasp information correctly when talking to people. They are super important at work because they make your conversations better. For example, let's say your co-worker explains a new project. If you are a good listener, you will get all the details right, understand what needs to be done, and can ask smart questions. This not only helps you but also makes your talks more efficient, which is a win-win! So, practice being a good listener for better communication on the job!

According to *The Oxford Dictionary*, Listening Skills can be defined as "The capacity to attentively focus on and accurately interpret what others are expressing". Listening is a valuable soft skill that plays a crucial role in how well we understand the information others share with us. It is one piece of the larger puzzle called communication skills, which includes not just listening but also speaking (verbal communication) and our ability to interact with others (interpersonal skills).

Imagine you are in a team meeting at work. Your colleague, Sarah, is giving a presentation on a new project. If you are a good listener, here's what happens:

1. **Active Engagement:** You are fully engaged in what Sarah is saying. You are not just hearing words; you are actively trying to understand her ideas, intentions, and the details of the project.
2. **Non-Verbal Cues:** Your body language shows that you are listening. You make eye contact, nod occasionally to show you are following along, and avoid distractions like checking your phone.
3. **Clarification:** If Sarah uses a term or concept you do not understand, you might ask a clarifying question. This shows that you are not just passive, but actively seeking to comprehend.
4. **Empathy:** When Sarah mentions the challenges the team might face, you empathize with her concerns. This empathy helps build rapport and trust.

5. Effective Response: After Sarah finishes, you respond with thoughtful questions and comments. You do not just regurgitate what she said, but you add value to the discussion.

By being a good listener in this scenario, you not only understand the project thoroughly, but you also contribute positively to the meeting. Your listening skills make you a better team player, enhance your professional relationships, and ultimately lead to more effective collaboration. In summary, listening is not just about hearing words; it is about actively engaging with the information, using non-verbal cues, seeking clarification, showing empathy, and responding effectively. These skills are invaluable in various aspects of life, especially in the workplace where clear communication is key to success.

2.15 Necessity of Developing Listening Skills

Listening skills are simply the ability to pay attention to what others are saying and understand their words. It is an essential skill. People have diverse motivations for listening:

- **To Acquire Information:** Listening is a way to gain new knowledge.
- **To Comprehend and Decode:** It helps in understanding the deeper meaning of what is being said.
- **For Pleasure and Learning:** Occasionally, we listen for enjoyment or to expand our knowledge.

However, focused listening can be challenging. Research suggests people remember only 25 per cent to 50 per cent of what they hear. But improving your listening skills can bring valuable benefits, especially in the business world. It aids in negotiations, client persuasion, conflict avoidance, and clearing misunderstandings—all crucial aspects of the business arena. Listening is not just a business tool; it is a cornerstone of communication. It reduces errors, boosts confidence, enhances popularity, sharpens leadership skills, and even helps in building a personal brand and expanding professional networks. Popularity and a strong personal brand are vital for success in the business world.

In a world filled with digital distractions and information overload, listening skills have suffered. It is essential to develop this life skill. During conversations, focus on one thing at a time. This helps understand the speaker, empathize with their perspective, build trust, and expand your professional network. Avoid distractions like muting your phone and maintain eye contact for full concentration. This not only fosters a positive impression but also confidence. Creating a positive impression happens quickly. Making eye contact makes the listener feel respected and confident. When a conversation begins, take time to find common ground and build a connection with the speaker.

Necessity/Importance Developing of Listening Skills

Listening skills are vital for effective communication. Communication consists of two parts: listening to others and expressing oneself. Often, people emphasize self-expression and forget the importance of listening. Here's why listening skills matter:

1. **Building Trust:** Listening recognizes the speaker's interests and builds trust. It connects people and validates their feelings, fostering openness in communication.

2. **Clearing Misunderstandings:** Misunderstandings can lead to serious consequences. Effective listening prevents errors and misunderstandings, especially in critical situations.

3. Conflict Avoidance: Poor communication triggers conflicts and misunderstandings. Hearing different perspectives promotes respect and defuses tense situations, vital in the business world.

4. Encouraging Empathy: Listening to others fosters empathy, helping you understand their situations better.

5. Enhancing Relationships: Effective listening strengthens business relationships, critical for project success and a company's reputation.

6. Boosting Productivity: Good listeners retain information and offer effective solutions, particularly in teamwork and group projects.

7. Improving Leadership: Listening improves leadership qualities by fostering better relationships with team members and avoiding misunderstandings.

In essence, listening skills are the foundation of successful communication and business relationships. They prevent misunderstandings, conflicts, and enhance productivity, making them invaluable in professional settings.

2.16 Techniques to Improve Listening Skills

Effective communication encompasses not only expressing ideas but also active listening. Just as honing your speaking abilities is valuable, improving your listening skills offers a multitude of benefits. Developing these skills enables you to extract more information from conversations, build trust with others, and make yourself more appealing through your attentive demeanor.

1. Project Inviting Body Language: Your body language significantly influences others' comfort and willingness to engage in conversation. Position yourself to encourage interaction by facing the speaker and maintaining an open posture. Avoid closed-off gestures like crossing your arms or displaying disinterest with excessive yawning or distracted glances.

2. Maintain Eye Contact: In many Western cultures, eye contact signifies engagement and respect. It signals your readiness to listen and encourages the speaker to continue.

3. Listen Without Distractions: Effective listening necessitates the ability to tune out background noise, internal thoughts, and other ongoing conversations to fully focus on the present discussion. Eliminating distractions, such as silencing your phone, keeps your attention on the speaker.

4. Pay Attention to Body Language: Beyond verbal content, body language conveys a wealth of information. Observe the speaker's gestures, posture, and facial expressions to gain deeper insights into their message.

5. Listen with a Learning Intent: Rather than immediately formulating your response while someone speaks, concentrate on absorbing and comprehending their message. Approach each conversation as an opportunity to learn and broaden your perspective.

6. Maintain an Open Mind: Refrain from forming judgements prematurely. Reserve your opinions until you have fully understood the speaker's perspective. Embrace the notion that others may perceive the world differently, and that diversity of thought is valuable.

7. Practice Empathy: Strive to understand and connect with the speaker's emotions. Empathizing allows for a deeper understanding of their viewpoint and feelings, even if you do not necessarily agree with them.

8. Refrain from Offering Immediate Solutions: When someone discusses a problem, resist the impulse to provide instant solutions. Sometimes, individuals simply want to be heard, and prematurely offering advice can hinder this process.

9. Use an Active-Listening Attitude: Cultivate an attitude that prioritizes listening as much as speaking in a conversation. Acknowledge that listening is vital for productive information exchange and is mutually beneficial for both—you and the speaker.

More Techniques

Here are the additional points along with the previous ones for improving listening skills.

10. Confirm the Statement: This step serves multiple purposes. It allows the speaker to correct any misunderstandings and ensures clarity in the conversation. Moreover, it encourages the speaker to delve into additional details or aspects that may not have been initially discussed.

11. Ask Questions: Asking questions is an effective technique to gain deeper insights into the speaker's perspective. The more questions you ask, the more comprehensive your understanding becomes.

12. Do not Interrupt: Allowing the speaker to express themselves without interruptions fosters a more productive and respectful conversation.

13. Listen for What They Do not Say: Sometimes, what's left unsaid can reveal as much as what is spoken. Pay attention to gaps or omissions in the conversation to gain a more holistic understanding.

14. Do not Jump to Conclusions: Avoid making assumptions based on your interpretation of words or phrases. Recognize that people may use language differently.

15. Do not React Too Noticeably: Maintain composure and objectivity, even if you have personal preferences or reservations about the speaker.

16. Do not Pre-judge: Avoid making assumptions about someone's character or abilities based on their appearance or background.

2.17 Principles of Listening Skills

To acquire listening skills, one needs to follow a few rules and principles, such as:

1. Maintain Silence (Resist the Urge to Speak): When engaged in a conversation, refrain from interrupting or speaking over others. Instead, actively listen to what they are saying, and only respond when they have finished speaking. For example, if a colleague is sharing their thoughts during a meeting, give them the floor to express themselves fully before chiming in with your ideas.

2. Mentally Prepare to Listen (Stay Focused): Concentration is key to effective listening. Clear your mind of distractions and truly focus on the speaker's message. Just as you would not let thoughts of lunch or your next appointment distract you, give the speaker your undivided attention. Imagine you are in a crucial business negotiation; your focus is on the deal, not external distractions.

3. Create a Welcoming Environment (Encourage Open Communication): Make the speaker feel comfortable sharing their thoughts. Use non-verbal cues like nods and maintain eye contact to signal your interest and openness. This approach fosters an atmosphere where people feel encouraged to express themselves. Think of it as creating a friendly space for productive dialogue in a team meeting.

4. Minimize Distractions (Eliminate External Interruptions): To enhance your listening, avoid activities that divert your attention, such as doodling or checking your phone during a conversation. These actions can send signals that you are disengaged. Treat listening as if you are watching a captivating movie; you would not want any interruptions then either.

5. Cultivate Empathy (Understand Different Perspectives): Empathizing with the speaker means trying to see things from their point of view. It requires setting aside your preconceived notions and biases. Much like a mediator in a dispute, remain impartial and genuinely try to grasp the speaker's perspective, even if you do not agree.

6. Exercise Patience (Allow for Natural Pauses): Do not rush the speaker. Pauses in speech are natural and often necessary for formulating thoughts. Give them the time they need to articulate their ideas. Picture yourself in a courtroom, where each person is given their turn to present their case without interruption.

7. Avoid Personal Bias (Stay Objective): Do not let personal quirks or habits of the speaker affect your perception of their message. Just as a judge in court must remain impartial regardless of the attorney's style, focus on the content of what's being said, not the delivery.

8. Listen to Tone (Recognize Vocal Cues): Pay attention to the speaker's tone of voice, as it conveys valuable information. A skilled public speaker adjusts volume and tone to emphasize points, just as a great actor does on stage. By tuning into these vocal cues, you can gain a deeper understanding of the speaker's emotions and intentions.

9. Comprehend the Bigger Picture (Connect the Dots): Effective listening involves piecing together information to grasp the speaker's overarching ideas. Much like solving a puzzle, focus on how individual points interconnect rather than just collecting isolated facts.

10. Observe Non-Verbal Signals (Read Gestures and Expressions): Remember that communication is not limited to words alone. Pay attention to body language, facial expressions, and eye movements, which often convey unspoken messages. It is akin to watching a silent film where the actions of the characters provide crucial insights.

2.18 Tips for Being a Good Listener

1. Stay Focused: When someone is talking to you, concentrate on their words. Put away distractions like your phone. Sometimes a WhatsApp message can distract you from the person right in front of you. For example, imagine your friend is sharing a story about their day. If you keep checking your phone, they might feel like you are not really listening.

2. Use Your Ears and Eyes: Pay attention not only to what's being said but also to the speaker's body language. Look into their eyes while they talk. This shows them that you are genuinely interested in what they have to say. For instance, when your teacher is explaining something, make sure you are looking at them. It helps you understand better and shows respect.

3. Avoid Making Assumptions: Let the speaker finish their thoughts before you jump in. Do not guess what they mean or finish their sentences for them. For example, if your friend mentions watching a show on Netflix, like "Indian Match Making," do not assume they hated it. They might have actually enjoyed it. Give them space to express themselves. Embrace moments of silence.

4. Listen First, Respond Later: Do not start planning your response while the speaker is talking. Often, we are so focused on what we are going to say next that we miss important details. Instead, just listen attentively. For instance, in a class discussion, focus on what your classmate is saying without immediately thinking about your reply.

5. Understand Different Perspectives: If you disagree with what's being said, try to see things from the speaker's point of view. Look for reasons why they might be right, not just where they are wrong. For instance, if someone has a different opinion on a movie, consider their viewpoint before stating your own.

6. Engage Actively: Show that you are tuned in by nodding or giving verbal cues like "I see" or "Go on". This lets the speaker know you are listening. For example, when your family member is sharing a story, nodding along can encourage them to continue.

7. Avoid Interruptions: Let the speaker finish their thoughts without cutting them off. Remember, this is not a TV debate; it is a conversation about your life and experiences.

8. Learn to be a Silent Listener: Sometimes, people just need someone to talk to. You do not always have to provide advice or solutions. Be comfortable with simply listening. You do not have to win every argument or have all the answers. Your friends might not be seeking advice; they might just want you to be there for them.

9. Demonstrate Your Active Listening: Use your body language and gestures to show that you are engaged in the conversation.

10. Offer Feedback: Our own biases and judgements can distort what we hear. As a listener, your role is to understand the speaker. This may involve reflecting on their words and asking questions to clarify their message.

Chapter Summary

Listening means using your ears to understand sounds when people talk. It's like your ears gather sounds—letters, rhythm, pauses—and your brain turns them into meaningful messages. Good listening is not just about the words; it is also about how they say it and what they show with their actions. Being a great listener involves focusing your mental processes, staying conscious and concentrated, treating it as a skill to practice, encouraging discussions, and paying attention to understand words deeply. Listening is like a smart brain job that becomes better with practice and makes your interactions with others more enjoyable and meaningful.

Listening is different from hearing. Hearing is passive, like sounds entering your ears without your control. Listening is active; it is when you really pay attention and concentrate on what you are hearing. Listening involves your brain, while hearing does not require much mental effort.

***The importance of listening cannot be overstated*:**

1. Builds Trust.
2. Reduces Misunderstandings.
3. Aids Conflict Resolution.
4. Fosters Empathy.
5. Improves Relationships.
6. Deepens Friendships.
7. Increases Productivity.
8. Facilitates Language Learning.
9. Enhances Leadership.
10. Empowers Others.
11. Solves Problems.
12. Avoids Being Judgemental.
13. Aids in Learning New Languages.

Effective listening means paying full attention, asking questions, and not interrupting or judging. Active listening is a valuable skill that fosters successful conversations in various settings, such as work, family, or social situations.

Benefits of Active Listening:

1. Builds Trust and Good Relationships.
2. Resolves Conflicts.
3. Prevents Missing Important Information.
4. Helps Spot Problems Early.
5. Enhances Learning.
6. Empowers the Listener.
7. Facilitates Making Friends and Providing Emotional Support.

Listening Involves Five Stages: hearing, understanding, remembering, evaluating, and responding.

Stage 1: Hearing—It's like your ears picking up sounds, but it is just the beginning.

Stage 2: Understanding—You piece together the message like solving a puzzle, understanding a movie plot, or following a recipe.

Stage 3: Remembering—Your brain stores the information, avoiding forgetfulness and distractions.

Stage 4: Evaluating—You act like a judge, sorting through facts, checking for truth, and seeing the big picture.

Stage 5: Responding—It's your turn to speak up, use non-verbal signals, keep the conversation flowing, and ask questions or comment.

Listening types include one-way and bilateral. One-way is message reception without feedback, like radio. Bilateral involves feedback, like live TV Q&A. Listening styles include active, appreciative, comprehension, critical, empathetic, relationship, sympathetic, and therapeutic listening.

Discriminative and informational listening are fundamental. Listener types vary from attentive and spontaneous to inattentive and imperative, with direct and indirect listening approaches. Each style and type has distinct characteristics and impacts on comprehension and learning. Importance of listening in the classroom includes creating a quiet environment, benefiting the mind, boosting self-assurance, supporting socio-emotional development, and improving academic success. Barriers to effective listening encompass physical and environmental factors like noise, juggling multiple conversations, and distractions. Psychological barriers, such as strong emotions or lack of interest, can hinder listening. Time pressure, rapid speech, tone, interruptions, bias, gender differences, lack of training, and poor listening habits are common barriers. Pseudo-listening and cognitive/ personal barriers also impact listening, requiring awareness and effort to overcome.

To overcome listening barriers: (1) Minimize distractions. (2) Prioritize listening. (3) Ask questions. (4) Listen carefully. (5) Reflect, do not redirect. (6) Manage information overload. (7) Avoid over-agreeing. (8) Combat faking attention. (9) Overcome emotional hurdles.

Listening skills are crucial for effective communication. They help you absorb information, build trust, and navigate the complexities of the business world. Techniques to improve these skills include using inviting body language, maintaining eye contact, avoiding distractions, paying attention to body language, and listening with a learning intent. It is essential to keep an open mind, practice empathy, and refrain from offering immediate solutions. Confirming statements and asking questions deepen your understanding, while avoiding interruptions and pre-judgements fosters respectful conversations. Remember, listening is as important as speaking in any dialogue. Developing these skills can lead to better communication, stronger relationships, and success in professional settings.

Principles of Listening Skills

1. Maintain silence; avoid interruptions.
2. Mentally prepare to listen and stay focused.
3. Create a welcoming environment with non-verbal cues.
4. Minimize distractions; eliminate external interruptions.
5. Cultivate empathy and understand different perspectives.
6. Exercise patience; allow for natural pauses.
7. Avoid personal bias and stay objective.
8. Listen to tone; recognize vocal cues.
9. Comprehend the bigger picture; connect the dots.
10. Observe non-verbal signals; read gestures and expressions.

Tips for Being a Good Listener

1. Stay focused; put away distractions.
2. Use your ears and eyes; pay attention to body language.
3. Avoid making assumptions; let the speaker finish.
4. Listen first, respond later; avoid planning your response.
5. Understand different perspectives; consider their viewpoint.
6. Engage actively with nods and cues.
7. Avoid interruptions; let the speaker finish their thoughts.
8. Learn to be a silent listener; sometimes people just need to talk.
9. Demonstrate active listening through body language.
10. Offer feedback by reflecting on their words and asking clarifying questions.

Questions

1. Mention any one definition of listening?
2. How does listening differ from hearing?
3. Why is listening important?
4. Explain the different types of listening with suitable examples.
5. Explain the different types of listeners with suitable examples.
6. Explain effective listening or active listening with an example.
7. What are the benefits of effective listening?
8. Discuss the stages of listening.
9. What are the barriers to listening?
10. How can listening barriers be overcome?
11. Explain the principles of listening skills.
12. What are the features of a good listener?

Chapter
3

Speaking Skills

3.1 Introduction

In the ever-evolving landscape of the twenty-first century, the ability to speak effectively has risen to prominence as one of the most essential skills. It transcends mere utility; it is, in fact, a life skill. The National Education Policy of 2020, attuned to the shifting demands of our times, underscores the pivotal role of communication skills in nurturing the holistic growth and development of our children. Within this framework, speaking emerges as a cornerstone among the productive communication skills. It is intriguing to note that while listening, reading, and writing can all be honed in isolation, the act of speaking inherently calls for the involvement of others. Indeed, the essence of speaking lies in its duality —a minimum of two participants engaging in the beautiful symphony of human communication. This journey begins in the cradle, where, under a mother's care, the first babblings of an infant mark the genesis of this innate ability. Yet, the spectrum of speaking skills extends far beyond the babblings of infancy. It encompasses a myriad of dimensions, weaving through the intricate tapestry of social interactions, academic pursuits, professional endeavours, and deeply personal moments. In social settings, the art of engaging in captivating conversations; in academia, the ability to articulate complex ideas with clarity; in the professional world, the power to persuade and inspire; and in the personal sphere, the capacity to forge connections and convey emotions —all these aspects converge under the umbrella of speaking skills. This chapter serves as an exploration, a journey through the multifaceted world of speaking and the cultivation of speaking skills. As we embark on this voyage, we shall unravel the intricacies, discover the nuances, and unearth the invaluable insights that empower us to become proficient and confident speakers in our ever-changing, communicative world.

3.2 Concept of Speaking

Speaking is not limited to mere talking. Speaking is an expressive skill. It's like having a friendly converse. It is each about participating studies and understanding each other. Suppose of it as talking to a friend casually. You do not just say anything aimlessly; you suppose about what to say and how to say it. That is what speaking is —it's like a two-way road, where you talk and hear. But it is not only about talking; it is also about listening and getting what others say. You should know when to talk, where to talk, why you are talking, and how to talk. It is a bit like knowing when to tell a funny story at a party or when to be serious in a meeting.

Webster's New World Dictionary defines speaking as the act of expressing words verbally, engaging in communication through speech, making requests, or delivering a formal speech. ***Hornby*** (1995, p. 20) elaborates that speaking encompasses discussing a topic, providing information, mentioning a subject, engaging in conversations, addressing someone using language, expressing oneself, or communicating in a specific language. According to ***Thornbury*** (2005, p. 121), speaking is like everyday talking when someone wants to share their thoughts with others. It happens naturally, not planned like a script. When people talk, they are sharing their ideas, information, or feelings. Speaking is like a team effort between two or more people who are talking together at the same time about something. As per *Cameron*, speaking is when you use your mouth and voice to show what you mean. It is something you can see and hear happening.

So, speaking is not just using words; it is using language the right way for the right time. It's like knowing the perfect moment to say commodity. That is why speaking is a precious skill—it is not only about what you say but also when and how you say it.

3.3 Concept of Speaking Skills

In the realm of language learning, several authors have shed light on the significance of speaking skills. ***Torky*** (2006) elucidates that speaking, one of the four language skills, involves producing and receiving information and is closely linked to listening as both are communication tools. ***Boonkit*** (2010) emphasizes the importance of speaking competence and confidence for effective communication, particularly in English as a Foreign Language (EFL) environments. ***Rao*** (2019) underscores the need to teach speaking skills comprehensively, detailing various speaking situations and advantages. ***Khan*** (2021) compares speaking proficiency among Bengali and English medium school students, highlighting the benefits of applying successful methods. ***Razaq*** (2022) explores the enhancement of speaking abilities by drawing on personal experiences, affirming that such experiences significantly contribute to speaking clarity among students. Collectively, these authors underscore the pivotal role of speaking skills and offer insights into effective strategies for their development in language learning contexts.

Mastering the art of speaking is a vital part of our communication toolkit, enabling us to connect with others and share our ideas and emotions. These speaking skills can be classified into formal and informal categories, each serving a unique purpose in different situations we encounter throughout our lives. Speaking skills encompass the ability to express information clearly and effectively through spoken words, ensuring that our message is comprehensible to those according to ***Bailey*** (2011), "Speaking is a productive oral skill consists of producing systematic verbal utterances to convey meaning ". Speaking goes beyond mere words; it is an engaging dance of constructing meaning through the exchange, production, reception, and processing of information, as described by scholars like Brown (1994) and Burns & Joyce (1997).

3.4 Features of Speaking Skills

Speaking is a language skill that plays a crucial role in the communication process. Through speaking skills, one can effectively convey thoughts, information, and ideas verbally. Here are some important features of speaking skills:

1. Vocabulary: Vocabulary is a fundamental aspect of speaking skills. To communicate effectively, one must expand their vocabulary in the language they wish to speak. For example, if you want to speak in English, you need to start by memorizing English vocabulary.

2. Grammar: While many people associate grammar primarily with writing, it is also an important aspect of speaking. Proper sentence structure and grammatical rules are essential for effective communication. Basic grammatical knowledge is necessary for speaking in any language.

3. Pronunciation: Good pronunciation is crucial for effective speaking. Clear and sufficiently loud speech is required for effective communication. Skilled speakers articulate their words clearly and project their voice so that the audience can hear them properly.

4. Fluency: Fluency is a key characteristic of effective speaking skills. To capture and maintain the audience's attention, a speaker must maintain a continuous and coherent flow of ideas throughout the speech.

5. Accuracy: Another important feature of speaking skills is accuracy. A speaker should strive for accuracy in sentence construction, pronunciation, the conveyance of information, and the tone of their voice.

6. Adaptability: Adaptability is a crucial aspect of speaking skills. Effective speakers need to adjust to the situation and circumstances of the event where they are delivering their speech. It is also important to connect with and adapt to the intellectual level of the audience.

7. Relationship with the Audience: Building a good relationship with the audience is essential for effective speaking. The speaker should establish positive connections on a personal, professional, and social level with the audience and others.

8. Self-Confidence: Speaking skills are closely associated with the self-confidence of the speaker. Self-confidence motivates speakers to engage in the speaking process. When the audience believes in the speaker, the speaker gains confidence and delivers the lecture with assurance.

Speaking skills enable the expression of ideas, thoughts, and body language, breaking down communication barriers.

It is a continuous process that involves practice, self-awareness, and a commitment to learning. In various aspects of life, speaking skills are respected and considered a meaningful activity.

3.5 Importance of Speaking Skills

1. Personal Fulfilment: When speakers connect with an audience who appreciates their well-prepared speech, they often experience a deep sense of satisfaction. This feeling of fulfilment is unique and not easily attained through other forms of communication.

2. Overcoming Nervousness: The usual nervousness that many people feel before speaking can transform into a sense of achievement and excitement when the audience shows appreciation. It's like a reward for all the effort and preparation put into refining speaking skills.

3. Boosting Confidence: Successful speaking experiences can boost a person's self-confidence. When you know you can deliver a good speech and people will appreciate it, you become more self-assured in various aspects of life.

4. Effective Communication: Speaking skills are not just about presenting well; they are also about communicating effectively in everyday life. Good speakers tend to express themselves clearly and persuasively, which helps them in personal relationships and social situations.

5. Problem-Solving: The ability to articulate your thoughts and ideas clearly is a valuable problem-solving skill. When you can express your thoughts effectively, you can find solutions to challenges more easily.

6. Leadership Development: Strong speaking skills are often a hallmark of effective leaders. Leaders need to inspire and influence others, and the ability to speak well is a key aspect of leadership.

7. Building Connections: Being a good speaker can help you connect with people on a deeper level. When you speak well, you can convey your feelings and ideas in a way that resonates with others, fostering stronger personal and professional relationships.

In summary, becoming a good speaker not only brings personal satisfaction but also helps you overcome nervousness, boosts your confidence, improves your communication abilities, enhances problem-solving skills, contributes to leadership development, and enables you to build meaningful connections with others. This skill is not limited to your career; it positively impacts various aspects of your life.

3.6 Types of Speaking Skills

There are different ways to speak, and each has its own goals. This helps you think clearly.

1. Discourse and Persuasive Speaking: This is about arguing, defending your ideas, and convincing others with good communication. It is helpful for thinking critically, understanding different views, and talking persuasively. You can get better at this by joining discussions, taking part in speaking classes, or practicing in mock debates.

2. Public Speaking Skills: This is about speaking to a big crowd. You need to talk clearly, use your body language well, and interest the audience. Good speaking builds confidence, leadership, and persuasion skills. Students can get better by joining speaking clubs, debating, or talking in front of classmates. It's like swimming; you learn by doing. Start small and grow.

3. Impromptu Speaking: Speaking without planning ahead is tough, it is called impromptu speaking. It means talking without getting ready first. You must think fast, get your ideas in order, and give a short, clear answer. To get better at this, you can practice impromptu speaking exercises or join real speaking contests. It helps you talk well even when you are in a hurry or under pressure.

4. Conversational skills: Talking with others is a big deal in our daily lives. Being good at it means you can join in on important chats, really listen, and speak your thoughts in a way that makes sense. These skills help you make friends and connect with people. If you are a student, you can get better at conversation by taking part in group talks, joining clubs or activities, and trying to hang out with others. It's like practicing to be a good talker and making more friends along the way.

5. Presentation Skills: Presentation Skills mean you can share information well using pictures and videos to keep people interested. Students often have to do presentations for school, and being good at this can make you do better in your classes and in your job later on. To get better at presentations, you can practice with example presentations, ask your friends or teachers for advice, and learn from people who are great at presenting things. It's like learning to tell a story with pictures and words, and it can help you succeed in your studies and work.

6. Interviewing Skills: Interviewing Skills are useful for both people in the interview. This includes asking questions, really listening, and the abilities you need for job and school interviews. Being able to answer questions well, being quick, and thinking carefully are all important. For job interviews, these skills can help you get the job you want, and for academic interviews, they can help you do well in school. It is like being good at having a chat with someone who wants to know more about you, or when you want to know more about them.

3.7 Effective Speaking Skills

Effective speaking means talking in a way that people understand and, if possible, act on what you say. There are two big parts to this: what you say and how you say it.

What You Say: This is about choosing the right words. The words you use when talking to a friend are different from what you would use in a formal presentation.

How You Say It: This is about how you speak, like whether you talk loud or soft and what your body language is like.

To speak effectively, you need to think about all these things. When you talk to a big conference about science, your kids about behaviour, or your boss about a raise, you want to make sure nothing distracts from your message.

The Main Features of Effective Speaking

1. The Words You Use: Your choice of words matters. It is different when you are talking to a big group, a colleague, your boss, or your children. Think about what they will understand.

2. Your Voice: Your voice can tell people a lot about you. If you are confident, your voice will show it. So, practice speaking well, especially if you need to talk in public.

A Quick Exercise: Record your own voice at home and listen to it. This can help you get used to your voice. Reading a document out loud can also help. Try it several times, and you will get better at it.

Breathing Matters: Your breath affects your voice. When you are stressed, your breathing changes, and that can make your voice sound different. Deep, calm breathing can help your voice sound better.

Body Language: More than half of what you communicate is non-verbal. It is not just what you say, but how you stand, your facial expressions, and gestures. Your non-verbal cues need to match your words for effective communication.

Remember, what you say and how you say it both matter for good communication. If they match up, people are more likely to understand and trust you.

3.8 Necessity of Developing Effective Speaking Skills

The Benefits of Developing Effective Speaking:

1. **Enhance Research Skills**
    - Preparing speeches helps you find and organize information, improving your research abilities.
    - You learn to identify credible information, which is valuable for various tasks, like product development, competitor analysis, or understanding industry trends.
2. **Advance Your Career**
    - Public speaking boosts credibility, helping your career.
    - Using these skills at work sets you apart and aids in presentations, meetings, and interviews.
3. **Build Confidence**
    - Public speaking boosts self-confidence by overcoming challenges.
    - Positive feedback empowers you, making you more comfortable in delivering speeches.
4. **Strengthen Critical Thinking**
    - Speech creation demands analysis and reflection, enhancing critical thinking.
    - Adjusting your speech based on audience reception sharpens this skill.
5. **Exercise Deductive Reasoning**
    - Deductive reasoning strengthens speeches, showing how you reached conclusions.

- It highlights thorough analysis, allowing the audience to agree or form their own conclusions.

6. **Represent Your Organization**
   - Public speaking represents your company, sharing its mission and improving marketing skills.
   - Speeches help potential customers understand your offerings, driving sales.
7. **Improve Oral Communication**
   - Speaking enhances oral communication skills through practice.
   - Feedback from colleagues and audience members improves speaking, also benefiting everyday conversations.
8. **Expand Your Network**
   - Speaking engagements expand your professional network.
   - Connections from events can lead to new opportunities or collaborations.
9. **Enhance Writing Skills**
   - Public speaking often involves speech writing, which hones your writing abilities.
   - Improved writing skills are useful for various tasks like reports, articles, and emails.
10. **Advocate for Causes**
    - Public speaking allows you to speak about topics you care deeply about.
    - You can inspire awareness and advocate for various issues or organizations.
11. **Develop Leadership Skills**
    - Speeches demonstrate leadership through information sharing and credibility.

- These skills can apply to other areas, such as leading meetings or group projects.

12. **Persuade and Inform**
    - Speaking empowers you to persuade and inform others on different subjects.
    - You can inspire change, collaboration, or learning in your audience.
13. **Utilize Performance Skills**
    - Speaking lets you use performance skills like timing, pace, and volume.
    - Intentional pauses and voice modulation make your speeches engaging.
14. **Expand Vocabulary**
    - Writing speeches introduces new words and helps eliminate filler words.
    - Adapting language to your audience enhances your communication.
15. **Encourage Change**
    - Public speaking motivates your audience to take action, such as a call to action at the end of your speech.
    - Effective speeches may lead to real change in your audience.
16. **Become a Better Listener**
    - Feedback after speeches improves listening skills.
    - You can apply feedback, identify audience interests, and become a more attentive listener when researching for speeches.

3.9 Tips for Developing Effective Speaking Skills

1. **Fluency**
    - Speak clearly, not too fast.

- Adjust your speaking pace based on the topic's complexity.
- Maintain a moderate volume, neither too quiet nor too loud.

2. Mistakes

- Do not fear making mistakes; everyone makes them.
- It is okay to correct yourself when you make a mistake.

3. Misunderstandings

- Do not panic if there is confusion; take a breath and try again.
- Some misunderstandings may cause laughter; embrace it, do not be embarrassed.

4. Practice

- Engage in conversations with various people.
- Do not limit discussions to academic topics; diverse topics are good practice.

5. Body Language

- Non-verbal communication, like gestures and facial expressions, is crucial.
- Pay attention to the body language and words of the person you are talking to.

6. Patience

- Stay positive; confidence grows with time.
- Realize that becoming an excellent speaker takes time, especially for non-native speakers.

7. Presentations and Public Speaking

- Avoid mumbling; use pauses and breaths instead of 'um' and 'ah'.
- Be yourself; do not copy someone else's style.
- Record yourself and work on a few areas for improvement.

8. **Communication Styles and Cultural Context**
   - Pay attention to common small talk topics if English is not your first language.
   - Feel free to use a lecturer's first name and ask direct questions if other students do the same.

3.10 Verbal Communication and Speaking Skills

Verbal communication means using words to tell others things. It can include speaking and writing. Some people only use "verbal communication" for speaking. Speaking clearly is important, but writing clearly is also vital, especially when there are no non-verbal clues to help. Verbal communication is talking to share information. It can be spoken or written. Communication is about telling something to someone else. This means that both the sender and the receiver are equally important. Verbal communication needs someone to talk or write (the sender) and someone to understand (the receiver). We will talk about both parts here.

There are many verbal communication skills. Some are easy to see, like speaking clearly and listening. Others are less obvious, like reflecting and clarifying. This page gives an overview of these skills and where to learn more. Remember that good verbal communication cannot be separated from non-verbal communication. Things like your body language, tone of voice, and facial expressions are important too. Talking clearly, staying calm, being polite, and following basic rules of manners help make verbal communication work better.

When you meet someone for the first time, the first few minutes are important. Your first impression is based on how they look, sound, and behave. It also depends on what you may have heard about them from others. This first impression guides your future conversations, to some degree. For example, if someone has an accent, you might use simpler words. If you know more about them, you might talk differently. Your first impression may change as you get to know the person better.

Speaking well has three main parts: the words you choose, how you say them, and how you use body language to support them. All of these affect how your message is understood by your audience. Choosing the right words is important. You may need different words for different situations, even when talking about the same thing. For example, talking to a close friend is different from speaking at a big conference. How you speak includes your tone and speed. These send important messages about your interest and emotions.

Listening actively is essential. When we communicate, we often think more about what we want to say than what the other person is saying. Good listening is important for effective verbal communication. Here are some ways to listen better:

- Be ready to listen. Focus on the speaker, not on what you will say.
- Stay open-minded and avoid making judgements.
- Understand what the speaker is saying overall, not just the details.
- Avoid distractions if possible.
- Be objective.
- Do not think of your next question while the other person is talking.
- Do not focus too much on one point.

Improving Verbal Communication: Advanced Techniques

You can use several tools and techniques to make your verbal communication better. These include reinforcement, reflection, clarification, and questioning.

Reinforcement is using encouraging words with non-verbal gestures like nods, a warm face, and eye contact. It helps build rapport and encourages openness in others.

Questioning helps you get information from others. There are closed questions that seek short answers and open questions that need more discussion.

Reflection is giving back your understanding of what someone said. It shows you care about their message and helps you check if you understood it right.

Summarizing is giving an overview of the main points or issues discussed. It helps review and agree on the message and plan next steps.

Ending a Conversation

How you end a conversation affects how it is remembered. You use verbal and non-verbal signals to close a conversation. Verbal signals include phrases like "I must be going" or "Thank you, that is helpful". Non-verbal signals include avoiding eye contact, standing up, or looking at a watch. People often start with non-verbal cues, especially face-to-face. On the phone, verbal cues are more important. Closing a conversation too quickly can stop the other person from finishing what they are saying. Make time to close the conversation. This is a good time to make future plans as well. Keep in mind that any communication includes many parts. Verbal communication is one of them, but it is essential. Spend time improving your verbal communication skills to communicate better.

3.11 Non-Verbal Communication and Speaking Skills

Communication usually means what we say—the words we use. But when we talk to people, it is not just about words. It also includes what we do not say with words. This is called non-verbal communication. Non-verbal communication is about what our body and voice say. It includes things like facial expressions, how we sound, gestures we make with our body (like waving our hands), and even how close or far we stand from someone when we talk. These non-verbal signals can tell us extra things that words alone cannot. Some experts think that 70 to 80 per cent of communication is non-verbal!

Non-Verbal Communication Helps Us

1. Say more or change what we say with our words. For example, when people nod their heads while saying "Yes," it shows they really agree.
2. Show how we feel. Our face, voice, and body can tell people how we feel, even if we do not talk. Have you ever asked someone if they are okay just because they looked sad?
3. Describe our relationship with someone. When you watch a couple talk, you might notice they do similar things with their body. They smile at the same time or move in the same way. This shows their connection.
4. Give feedback to the other person. Smiling and nodding show that you are listening and agree. Hand movements might show you want to talk. These signals give information without words.
5. Control the flow of our talk. We use signs to show we are done talking or that we want to speak. For example, nodding and closing our lips show we are finished speaking. Making eye contact and a small nod can show we want to speak.

Learning the Language

Some people say non-verbal communication is like a language

you can learn. If we knew the meaning of every nod, look, and gesture, we could understand how people feel and what they want. But it is not that easy. Non-verbal communication is not fixed like a language with set rules. It changes depending on the situation. Where you are, who you are with, and the culture all matter. For example, nodding your head at a meeting might mean something different than nodding at someone across a room. And it is different when you are having a friendly chat. Sometimes, our body speaks without us knowing it. We might try to show one thing with our body and another with our words. It is hard to understand non-verbal communication by itself. It is part of the whole communication package, along with what we say (verbal communication).

Non-Verbal Communication in Writing

Some people say written words also have non-verbal communication. Handwriting can show your mood when you write a note. And now, things like font and colour can say something about you.

But these are not as reliable as non-verbal communication in person. They show less than non-verbal signals you give face-to-face.

The Cultural Context

Most people learn to understand non-verbal communication as they grow up. It is a normal part of how we talk to others. We use and understand it without thinking. But non-verbal communication is culture-specific. This means it can be different in different cultures. For example, in some countries, people use big gestures, lots of hand-waving, and loud talking to show excitement. In other countries, it is more subtle. The way you use gestures and body language depends on the culture. For example, a thumbs-up means approval in English-speaking countries, but it is rude in some other places.

Types of Non-Verbal Communication

1. Body Movements (Kinesics): This is all about the movements we make with our bodies, like gestures or nods. For example, waving your hand to say hello is a body movement that adds meaning to your words. When someone shakes their head while saying "yes," it can create confusion because their body movement contradicts their words.

2. Posture: How you stand or sit, whether your arms are crossed or relaxed, all send non-verbal signals. For instance, slouching might show that you are feeling tired or uninterested. Imagine someone sitting up straight with a serious expression during a meeting; their posture signals attentiveness and engagement.

3. Eye Contact: The amount of eye contact you make can tell a lot about your trustworthiness and your level of interest in a conversation. Maintaining good eye contact shows you are engaged. During a job interview, making consistent eye contact with the interviewer demonstrates confidence and sincerity.

4. Para-Language: This refers to things in your voice other than your actual words, like the pitch, tone, and speed of your speech. If you speak very slowly, it might indicate that you are not excited about the topic. If someone talks rapidly and with excitement when discussing their hobbies, it conveys their passion for those activities.

5. Personal Space (Proxemics): Your comfort zone when it comes to personal space can vary a lot by culture. Some people are okay with close conversations, while others prefer more space. In some cultures, people stand closer together during conversations, while in others, maintaining more physical distance is the norm.

6. Facial Expressions: Your face often reveals your emotions. A big smile typically means happiness, while a furrowed brow may signal confusion or concern. When someone's face lights up with a smile upon receiving a thoughtful gift, it shows their joy and appreciation.

7. Physiological Changes: These are things happening in your body, like sweating or a faster heartbeat. When you are nervous, your body might give you away through these changes. A person's sweaty palms and increased heart rate before a public speaking event can indicate their nervousness, even if they try to hide it verbally.

3.12 Public Speaking

Public speaking skills have become increasingly crucial in today's fast-paced world, where effective communication can open doors to personal and professional success. The ability to address a substantial audience during various occasions is a valuable asset. Public speaking is not confined to any particular field; it is relevant in education, politics, social work, business, and virtually all aspects of life. Engaging in effective public speaking offers a multitude of benefits. It allows individuals to connect with and influence a large gathering of people. Through the power of words, one can convey their thoughts, ideas, and perspectives, leaving a lasting impact on their audience. This ability to articulate and express oneself is not only valuable but also essential for those who wish to lead, inspire, or educate others.

Public speaking is both an art and a skill. It involves more than just stringing words together—it requires mastery of the spoken language, vocal modulation, body language, and the ability to convey emotions effectively. The artistry lies in engaging the audience, creating a connection through shared emotions and building a sense of affection and rapport. Skilled public speakers can take a diverse group of individuals and make them feel united in purpose. Moreover, public speaking is not limited to formal presentations or speeches. It plays a pivotal role in everyday life, whether you are delivering a business proposal, addressing a community issue, or even participating in a casual conversation. The capacity to communicate effectively is a tool that can enhance your personal and professional growth, offering countless opportunities for advancement.

In essence, public speaking is not just a skill; it is a gateway to building relationships, fostering understanding, and influencing others positively. It is a versatile asset that can significantly contribute to your success and help you thrive in various spheres of life. Therefore, honing your public speaking abilities is a valuable investment in your future.

3.12.1 *Meaning of Public Speaking*

Public speaking means talking in front of a big group of people. When you give a public speech, you are trying to do different things like teaching, making people happy, or convincing them of something. Sometimes, you use pictures or slideshows to help explain things and make the speech more interesting. According to ***Merriam Webster Dictionary:*** Public speaking is the art of effective oral communication with an audience.

Public speeches are different from online presentations because they are live and happen at a specific time and place. Online presentations can be watched whenever you want. Some ancient cultures, like Egypt, had folks learning how to do public speaking, and it is been around for a long time. Today, public speaking has changed a lot because of technology. We now have things like video calls and fancy presentations that make it different from how it used to be.

3.12.2 *Benefits of Public Speaking*

Let's break down the benefits of public speaking in really easy terms:

1.Career Boost: Public speaking skills can help your job. It shows you are smart, confident, and professional. You can even add it to your resume. It helps in meetings and job interviews.

2. Confidence: Speaking in public can make you feel brave. Even if you are scared at first, it helps you grow. This confidence is useful everywhere, like at work or on a date.

3. Thinking Smart: When you make a speech, you have to think a lot. How to talk so people understand? This kind of thinking makes you better at talking with others in everyday life.

4. Better Communication: Making speeches helps you talk better. In your personal life or at work, you will be a better communicator.

5. New Friends: After your speech, people will want to talk to you. It is easier to make friends and business contacts.

6. Personal Satisfaction: Even if it is scary, speaking in public shows you can do it. It feels good when you overcome your fears.

7. More Network: Speaking at events helps you meet lots of people. You can also connect with other speakers.

8. Learn to Persuade: Public speaking can inspire people to take action. You can make a difference.

9. Leadership: It helps you speak your mind and change minds. Leadership often needs good speaking skills.

10. Performance Skills: Speaking teaches you how to talk with good timing and variety. You will also learn acting skills like using props.

11. Better Vocabulary: You will know which words to use and be more confident in your speech.

12. No Fear of Impromptu Speaking: You would not worry if you have to speak suddenly at a wedding or special event.

13. Learn to Argue: Preparing for speeches makes you good at making strong arguments.

14. Drive Change: Speaking in public can make a big impact. You reach many people at once.

15. Be a Better Listener: Attending speeches makes you better at listening.

All these benefits make public speaking worth trying, even if you are nervous at first. You will learn to enjoy it!

3.12.3 *Elements of Public Speaking*

Public speaking is like talking to a bunch of people without showing that you are nervous. Even when you are in a meeting, on a phone call, or explaining things to your boss, you are doing a bit of public speaking. Let's dig into the seven elements of public speaking, which are super important when you talk to folks.

1. The Speaker: You, the person talking, are super important. It is not just about the slides or props you use; it is how you express yourself. Your motivation, speaking skills, and style matter.

2. The Message: This is what you are saying, both in words and how you say them. Think about what you talk about, how you talk, and the way you structure your speech.

3. The Audience: Before you speak, figure out who you are talking to. Are they young, old, where are they from, what do they do? Your talk should fit them like a glove.

4. The Channel: Whether it is a microphone or a video call, the way your voice or video reaches people is crucial. If it is not clear, your message can get messed up.

5. Feedback: This is when you hear what the crowd thinks and respond to them. It is not just about you talking; it is about you and your audience understanding each other.

6. The Noise: There are two kinds of noise to watch out for. Internal noise happens when you are confused. External noise can be laughter, bad air, or anything that distracts. To fight noise, use different ways of talking, make sure the place is ready for speaking, and repeat your ideas.

7. The Place or Situation: Where you talk is super important. You need to check the spot beforehand, like the seats, lights, and even the temperature, so that everything's perfect.

So, public speaking is not just about talking; it is a whole set of things you need to get right to do it well. Whether you are giving a big speech or chatting with your boss, these elements matter.

3.12.4 *Preparing a Public Speaking*

Following steps can be taken for preparing a public speaking:

1. **Know Your Audience**
    - Understand who you are speaking to.
    - Use language, speech length, and topics suitable for your audience.
2. **Familiarize Yourself with the Environment**
    - Visualize where you will speak.
    - Check if you need a stage, podium, or microphone.

- Plan your route to the location.

3. **Outline the Main Points**
   - Create a structured outline.
   - Use keywords to remember key points.
4. **Have Someone Review Your Speech**
   - Get feedback from a trusted friend or co-worker.
   - Make improvements based on their suggestions.
5. **Practice on Your Own**
   - Time yourself to fit the allocated duration.
   - Use notecards initially, then rely on them only when needed.
6. **Incorporate Hand Gestures**
   - Use hand movements to engage and remember content.
7. **Use a Mirror:**
   - Practice in front of a mirror to refine your delivery.
8. **Record Yourself**
   - Record your practice sessions and review them for improvement.
9. **Rehearse in Front of Someone**
   - Try your speech with a small audience for comfort.
10. **Use the Stage**
    - Move around if you have a large audience to engage everyone.
11. **Anticipate Questions**
    - Prepare answers to expected questions from the audience.
12. **Prepare Your Equipments**
    - Ensure all technical equipment is working correctly.

Following these steps can help you feel confident and deliver a compelling presentation, no matter the type of public-speaking event you are facing.

3.12.5 *Tips for Developing Effective Public Speaking Skills*

Many people fear public speaking, but there are ways to calm those nerves and become a memorable speaker. Here are a few tips to enhance your public speaking:

1. **Nervousness is Normal, so Prepare**
    - Feeling nervous is normal; it can make you alert.
    - Prepare thoroughly; practice and get feedback from friends.
2. **Know Your Audience**
    - Tailor your speech to your audience.
    - Learn about your listeners to choose words and content accordingly.
3. **Organize Your Material**
    - Create a structured framework for your speech.
    - Grab the audience's attention in the first 30 seconds.
4. **Adapt to Audience Feedback**
    - Stay focused on the audience's reactions.
    - Adjust your message to keep them engaged.
5. **Let Your Personality Shine**
    - Be yourself; do not sound robotic.
    - Authenticity builds credibility and trust.
6. **Use Humour, Tell Stories, and Effective Language**
    - Inject humour and anecdotes.
    - Personal stories can engage your audience.
7. **Do not Read, Work from an Outline**
    - Avoid reading from scripts.
    - Maintain eye contact for better connection.
8. **Use Voice and Hands Effectively**
    - Non-verbal cues are vital.
    - Convey ideas clearly without distractions.

9. Start Strong, End Stronger

- Avoid dull openings like announcing your topic.
- Begin with a surprising fact or quote and close with a memorable statement.

10. Use Audio-visual Aids Wisely

- Use visual aids sparingly.
- Ensure they enhance your message and engage your audience.

Remember, perfect communication does not exist, but preparation can significantly improve your public speaking skills and reduce anxiety.

3.12.6 *Types of Public Speaking*

Public speaking is the art of using words to communicate with an audience. It can be done in various settings, from small gatherings to large televised events. To master public speaking, it is crucial to understand the four primary types of public speaking: ceremonial, demonstrative, informative, and persuasive.

1. Ceremonial Speaking: Ceremonial speeches are given on special occasions like weddings, graduations, funerals, and even festive parties. They often involve toasts and have a personal, emotional connection with the audience. These speeches mark significant moments in people's lives.

2. Demonstrative Speaking: Demonstrative speaking focuses on explaining and showing how something is done. It often involves science demonstrations or role-playing to illustrate a process. The key is to speak clearly and concisely while demonstrating actions, ensuring the audience gains practical knowledge.

3. Informative Speaking: Informative speaking is about explaining a concept or providing factual information to the audience. It is commonly seen in college lectures, industry conferences, and when public officials share vital information. The primary goal here is to disseminate information, not necessarily to persuade or demonstrate.

4. Persuasive Speaking: Persuasive speaking is often dramatic and is used by politicians, lawyers, and clergy members. It involves convincing the audience to adopt a particular viewpoint. This type of speaking requires mastering voice inflections and language nuances to emotionally appeal to the audience and use strong language.

A speech presentation typically includes an introduction, a main body with key points, and a conclusion. The type of speech (informative, persuasive, or motivational) depends on the goal of the presentation. Informative speeches provide facts, persuasive speeches aim to influence opinions, and motivational speeches seek to inspire and encourage action.

The effectiveness of a speech presentation is greatly influenced by the speaker's delivery. This includes maintaining eye contact, using voice inflection and facial expressions to engage the audience, and occasional gestures to emphasize key points. While movement during a speech can be effective, it is essential not to overdo it.

3.13 Extemporaneous Speech

Extempore, extemporaneous, and impromptu speaking are similar and can be used interchangeably. The word "extempore" comes from the Latin phrase "Ex tempore," which means speaking without preparation. This type of speaking is about our ability to adapt to unexpected and changing situations in life.

3.13.1 *Concept of Extemporaneous Speech*

In general, extempore speaking involves addressing an audience without prior preparation. It is a form of public speaking in which the speaker presents a topic without prior rehearsal or practice. The speaker receives the topic for their speech just before the event, and they must think quickly and present it in an organized manner to the audience, often including personal insights or comments. According to the ***Oxford Dictionary***, "Extempore is spoken, done, or written without any prior preparation or thought". Extempore is often used to assess people's ability to think on their feet and present their thoughts coherently about current events. For example, debates and job interview topics often require extempore speaking skills.

3.13.2 *Presentation of Extemporaneous Speech*

If you ever find yourself in a situation where you need to give an unplanned speech in front of others, here's a step-by-step guide to help you through it:

1. **Gather Your Thoughts**
   - First, take a moment to collect your ideas. Think about the main point you want to convey. What's the most important thing you need to say?
2. **Express Gratitude**
   - Begin by thanking the person who asked you to speak. This shows appreciation for the opportunity and sets a positive tone.
3. **Deliver Your Message**
   - Now, it is time to speak. Share your main points as succinctly as possible while ensuring that you cover it well. Speak at a pace that your listeners can easily follow. Remember, clarity is key.

4. **Show Gratitude Again**
   - After you have made your point, thank the person once more for giving you the chance to speak. This demonstrates respect and professionalism.
5. **Conclude**
   - Finally, once you have delivered your message and expressed your gratitude, it is time to stop talking. A well-structured and concise speech is often more impactful than a lengthy one.

In summary, when you have to speak on the spot, take a moment to gather your thoughts, thank the person who invited you, deliver your main point clearly, thank them again, and conclude your speech. These steps can help you navigate an impromptu speaking situation with confidence.

3.13.3 *Benefits of Extemporaneous Speech*

1. Flexibility: Extempore speaking is super flexible. That means the speaker can change things up to fit the audience and the situation. This makes the speech more interesting and engaging for the listeners.

2. Authenticity: Extempore speeches sound natural. The speaker is not reading from a script, so it feels like a friendly chat. This helps the speaker connect with the audience on a personal level.

3. Better Communication Skills: People who practice extempore speaking get really good at explaining things clearly. They learn how to organize their thoughts on the spot and answer tricky questions.

4. Quick Thinking and Problem-Solving: Extempore speaking makes your brain work fast. You have to think on your feet, evaluate ideas, and give smart answers. It's like a mental workout.

5. Boosted Confidence: When you get good at extempore speaking, your confidence goes up. You start to believe in your knowledge and speaking abilities. This helps you in all kinds of conversations.

Extempore speeches are popular because they sound informal and show the speaker knows their stuff. When you know a topic really well, you speak calmly and confidently, making the audience trust you. Plus, you can pause and answer questions from the audience, making sure everyone understands. The best part is you can add stories or examples that just happened, like something said by a previous speaker. It keeps your speech fresh and engaging. That is why extempore speaking is such a great method.

3.14 Group Discussion

In common sense, a group is a collection of two or more individuals who interact and put in effort to achieve a common interest. When two or more individuals exchange information and thoughts in a face-to-face situation to achieve goals, that is a group discussion. It is a form of social interaction where individuals discuss a specific topic or problem to gain a better understanding. Generally, the group discussion process is used in educational, professional, and guidance sectors. It aims to reach a unanimous decision based on the opinions of a group of people.

3.14.1 *Concept of Group Discussion*

Group discussion is a formal conversation where people are divided into several groups to discuss a specific topic. Through this process, institutions evaluate individuals' personality traits and skills in a group setting. The ability to discuss, debate, and question are important outcomes of group discussion.

It helps us address common concerns and understand the concept of the topic by considering numerous opinions and information. Group discussion is democratic in nature and encourages open-minded ideas. It is conducted in an open and respectful environment where people accept others' opinions with dignity and do not let personal biases interfere. According to the ***Merriam-Webster Dictionary (Online):*** "a discussion involving a number of people who are connected by some shared activity, interest, or quality". On the other hand, ***Study.com*** clarifies that a discussion group is a conversation about a particular topic, text, or issue taking place within a group. The keyword here is "discussion". A group discussion is not a lecture, a class, or an argument. It involves a group of people actively listening and responding to a subject.

3.14.2 *Features of Group Discussion*

1. Clear Objective: In a group discussion, it is important to have a clear goal. This helps participants focus and work together to achieve that goal. Typically, someone initiates the discussion by stating its purpose.

2. Motivated Interaction: When group members are motivated, they are more willing to put the group's interests ahead of their own. This motivation leads to more productive discussions.

3. Logical Organization: Participants need to decide how they will structure the discussion, exchange views, and reach a group consensus. Without a plan, a few members might dominate the conversation, making it less meaningful.

4. Friendly Atmosphere: Creating a cooperative and friendly environment prevents conflicts between group members.

5. Effective Communication: Good communication is crucial for a successful group discussion. This includes clear speech, simple language, and the right tone. Paying attention to non-verbal cues, like body language, is also important.

6. Participation by All: It is important for every member to participate. Encouraging each other's involvement makes the group discussion more effective.

7. Leadership Qualities: Effective leaders initiate discussions, present ideas logically, encourage everyone's participation, and summarize the conversation.

8. Interaction: Group discussions involve members talking, listening, and communicating with each other. They share ideas and information during the discussion.

9. Conflict: Disagreements or conflicts among group members are common during discussions. They often occur when there are different solutions to a problem. While conflict can be a good thing, as it can lead to new solutions, it can also be disruptive if it arises from political behaviours within the group.

10. Collaboration and Teamwork: Group discussion always encourages collaboration and teamwork. The participants in a group discussion interact to achieve a common interest and goal. Without cooperation and collaboration, a group discussion cannot be fruitful.

3.14.3 *Types of Group Discussion*

Let's break down and simplify the types of group discussions:

1. Topic-Based Discussions: In this type of group discussion, participants talk about a given topic. During job interviews, candidates might get a list of topics to choose from for discussion. The final topic to discuss is usually decided by the group members, based on what they all agree on. The topics can be anything, from real-life facts to more abstract ideas.

Example: In a job interview, candidates might be asked to discuss topics like "The Impact of Technology on Society" or "Teamwork in the Workplace". They pick one topic to talk about together.

2. Timing of the Topic: The topic for discussion can be given to participants in two ways. It can either be told to them before the discussion date (pre-announced) or right on the spot. When topics are pre-announced, it gives participants time to prepare their thoughts. On the other hand, on-the-spot topics check how well participants can think quickly. In these cases, participants are usually given five to ten minutes to gather their thoughts.

Example: In a school debate, students might know the topic in advance, like "Climate Change". But in a spontaneous classroom discussion, the teacher might suddenly ask them to talk about "The Benefits of Reading".

3. Case-Based Discussions: Sometimes, participants are given a specific case to discuss. This case can be a real-life situation or a made-up scenario. At the end of the case, participants are asked a few questions. Everyone in the group is expected to carefully analyse the case and come up with the most logical and creative solutions to the questions.

Example: In a business meeting, employees might discuss a real case where the company faced a challenge, and they are asked how to overcome it. Or in a classroom, students might be given a hypothetical case about solving a community problem and asked to come up with solutions.

These types of group discussions help people share their ideas, solve problems, and make decisions together. They can happen in different settings, like schools, workplaces, or even social gatherings.

3.14.4 *Group Discussion in Classroom*

Group Discussion (GD) plays a vital role in today's classroom learning. The way we teach and learn has changed over time. Now, it is not just about the teacher talking; it is more about the students being involved in their learning. We use modern methods like Flip learning, GD, PowerPoint Presentations, and Smart Classrooms to keep students engaged while the teacher teaches. GD, in particular, offers several advantages. It encourages students to think, be active in a group, share their thoughts, and work together to solve problems. This makes the classroom lively, boosts students' confidence, and helps them overcome shyness to become active team players.

In simpler terms, GD is like a friendly chat in the classroom. It is not just the teacher talking all the time; it is about students talking to each other and learning together. Here's why it is great:

1. **Sharing Ideas:** In GD, students get to say what they think about a topic. They can share their ideas and see what their classmates think too. It's like a big brainstorming session.
2. **Teamwork:** GD helps students work together as a team. They discuss and find solutions to problems as a group. This teamwork skill is super important in school and in life.
3. **Building Confidence:** Talking in a group can be scary, but GD helps students become more confident. It's like practice. The more they talk, the more confident they become.
4. **Overcoming Shyness:** Some students might be shy and not like talking in front of the class. GD helps them overcome that shyness. They realize it is okay to share their thoughts.

So, GD is a cool way to learn together in a classroom. It's like having a friendly conversation with your classmates, but you are also learning and becoming more confident at the same time. It is a win-win for students and teachers!

3.14.5 *Types of Group Discussion in Classroom*

There are various methods of group discussion used in the classroom setting. These methods can be broadly classified into two categories: (1) Formal Discussion and (2) Non-Formal Discussion.

1. Formal Discussion: This type of group discussion process in the classroom involves pre-planned and controlled aspects. Here, the teacher plans and directs the discussion. Teachers follow a predetermined plan to guide the discussion. Some methods of formal group discussion in a classroom setting include:

(a) **Panel Discussion:** In a panel discussion, a problem or topic is selected in advance. The topic is announced before the discussion begins. Students are divided into several groups, each with a leader. Panel members discuss the topic and raise questions. The teacher moderates the discussion, ensuring that everyone participates and maintaining order.

(b) **Symposium:** In Ancient Greece, they had something called a "symposium" as part of their fancy dinners. After eating, people would gather to have fun. They would listen to music, dance, hear stories, and chat. Some famous Greek writings, like Plato's Symposium and Xenophon's Symposium, talk about or happen during these parties. Greek poems, like Theognis of Megara's poems, also mention them. You can even see pictures of these parties in old Greek and Etruscan art.

Now-a-days, a "symposium" is like a meeting or conference where people come together to talk about something. It is often a public event where people in the audience listen to presentations. In classrooms, students pick a topic, talk about it in front of their classmates, and have a discussion about it. They write down important points as they go along.

(c) **Debate:** In a debate, you have two teams. Each team has a different opinion about a topic, like "Should we have more recess at school?" or "Is technology good for kids?" One team thinks, "Yes," and the other team thinks, "No". The teacher is like the referee; they make sure the debate is fair and follow the rules. Each team takes turns to talk. One person from the "Yes" team talks about why they think it is a good idea, and then someone from the "No" team explains why they disagree. They go back and forth, taking turns. To win the debate, it is not about being loud; it is about being smart. You have to say logical things that make sense. It's like giving good reasons for your ideas. And, you need to speak clearly and without stumbling over words. This is what we mean by "fluency". The teacher listens carefully to both teams. They decide who did the better job. It is not about which side is right; it is about who made the stronger argument. The debate helps you learn how to talk about important issues and how to listen and think carefully. It's like a fun and educational game where everyone gets a chance to speak their mind.

2. Non-Formal Discussion: In non-formal discussions, teachers and students can talk freely without a strict plan. They share their thoughts and ideas. Everyone in the classroom can join in, and the teacher keeps an eye on things. This means the teacher should know a lot about the topic they are talking about. It's like having a chat where everyone can talk and share their ideas without strict rules.

3.14.6 *Merits of Group Discussion in Classroom*

Group discussions in the classroom have several definite merits:

1. **Active Learning:** Group discussions in the classroom make learners more active. Being actively engaged in learning helps them remember things for the long term.

2. **Idea Generation:** These discussions help generate new and innovative ideas by considering different viewpoints, leading to novel problem-solving approaches.

3. **Social Development:** Group discussions foster the social development of students, allowing them to acquire important social skills and virtues.

4. **Boosting Confidence:** Participating in group discussions boosts learners' self-confidence as they express their thoughts in front of others and receive approval and feedback.

5. **Teacher-Student Relationship:** Group discussions are beneficial for developing a healthy and positive relationship between teachers and students. It affects positively throughout the session.

3.14.7 *Limitations of Group Discussion in Classroom*

1. **Not Everyone Talks:** In group discussions, some kids might talk a lot, while others stay quiet. This means not everyone gets a chance to share their ideas. It's like some voices are loud, and others are soft.

2. **Feeling Pressured:** Sometimes, kids in a group might feel like they have to agree with the loud kids. This can make them say things they do not really think. It's like being pushed

to follow the crowd, and it stops them from speaking their true thoughts.

3. Getting Distracted: Group discussions can go off track. People might start talking about different stuff or not pay attention. This messes up the conversation and makes it harder to learn from it.

4. Disagreements: When kids talk in groups, they might not always agree. It is okay to have different ideas, but if they cannot work it out, it can lead to arguments and hurt feelings. This can break the friendly feeling in the group.

5. Not Enough Time: Group discussions are often timed, so there is not a lot of time for each person to speak. This means some people might not get to say all they wanted, and the talk feels rushed.

So, group discussions can have some problems, like not everyone speaking, feeling pressured, getting off-topic, arguing, and running out of time.

3.15 Barriers to Speaking Skills

1. Lack of Confidence: One common barrier to speaking skills is a lack of confidence. Many people feel nervous when they have to speak in front of an audience. They worry about making mistakes, and this fear can hold them back from speaking effectively.

2. Reserved Nature: Some individuals are naturally reserved. Their reserved nature can hinder them from expressing their thoughts in social gatherings or speaking in public. They may find it challenging to open up in front of others.

3. Limited Vocabulary: Having a limited vocabulary is another significant barrier to speaking skills. If you do not know enough words, it can affect your fluency and confidence when speaking to people. A rich vocabulary is essential for effective communication.

4. Pronunciation Issues: Clear and loud pronunciation is crucial for good speaking. Poor pronunciation can disrupt the clarity and understanding of your message. To engage your audience, you need to articulate words clearly and with sufficient volume.

5. Speaking Too Quickly: Speaking too quickly can make it difficult for the audience to understand. It can blur the words and create confusion. Effective communication requires a moderate speaking pace for better comprehension.

6. Grammar Challenges: Proper grammar is essential for effective communication. Sound knowledge of grammar rules and sentence construction is necessary to make your speech meaningful and engaging. Incorrect sentences can diminish the impact of your speech.

7. Lack of Practice: Finally, a lack of practice is a significant barrier to speaking skills. Speaking skills improve with practice. If you want to become proficient in speaking, you need to practice regularly. Simply having a good vocabulary and knowing grammar is not enough; practice is key to delivering successful speeches.

8. Inadequate Use of Gestures: Gestures refer to the movements of our limbs that enhance verbal communication. During a speech, it is important that these gestures align with the words being spoken. Overuse or incorrect utilization of gestures can detract from the impact of the speech and disengage the audience.

9. Unfavourable Environment: The environment for a speech encompasses things like the room size, lighting, seating, and temperature. This setting can greatly affect how well a speech goes. If there are issues with the surroundings, it can hinder the delivery of a successful speech.

Overcoming these barriers involves building confidence, expanding your vocabulary, practicing pronunciation, and improving grammar. It is important to remember that speaking is a skill that can be developed and enhanced over time with dedication and practice.

3.16 Remedies for Overcoming Speaking Barriers

1. **Talk with Others:** To improve your speaking skills, engage in conversations with people you know.
2. **Seek Help:** Have discussions with teachers and classmates about any difficulties you have when speaking in front of others.
3. **Practice:** Keep practicing. Record your speeches, listen to them, make improvements, and practice some more.
4. **Use Stories:** Begin your speech with an interesting story to capture your audience's attention.
5. **Embrace Mistakes:** Remember, it is okay to make mistakes; everyone does. Do not be afraid of making errors.
6. **Learn from Experts:** Pay attention to your favourite speakers. Observe their gestures, tone of voice, pronunciation, and word choice, and try to emulate them.

Chapter Summary

Speaking is not just talking. It is expressing, like talking with a friend. Think before you speak. It is also about listening, adapting, and being confident. Good speaking means using the right words and grammar, clear pronunciation, a smooth flow of ideas, accuracy, and building a connection with the audience. It breaks communication barriers and is valuable in life. Speaking skills are important for personal fulfilment, overcoming nervousness, boosting confidence, effective communication, problem-solving, leadership development, and building connections. These skills impact various aspects of life, not just career. There are six types of speaking skills:

1. **Discourse and Persuasive Speaking:** Defending ideas and convincing others, useful for critical thinking and persuasion.
2. **Public Speaking:** Talking to a large audience, building confidence, leadership, and persuasion.
3. **Impromptu Speaking:** Speaking without prior preparation, helps in quick, clear responses under pressure.
4. **Conversational Skills:** Essential for daily interactions, making friends, and connecting with people.
5. **Presentation Skills:** Sharing information effectively using visuals, crucial for school and work success.
6. **Interviewing Skills:** Important for job and academic interviews, including asking questions, active listening, and quick thinking.

Effective Speaking involves both what you say and how you say it, and aligning these elements is key to ensuring people understand and trust you. Developing effective speaking skills offers numerous benefits, including enhancing research abilities, advancing your career, building confidence, strengthening critical thinking, representing your organization, improving oral communication, expanding your network, enhancing writing skills, advocating for causes, developing leadership skills, persuading and informing, utilizing performance skills, expanding your vocabulary, encouraging change, becoming a better listener, and more. To improve your speaking skills, it is important to speak clearly, adjust your pace based on the topic's complexity, embrace mistakes and misunderstandings, practice diverse topics, pay attention to body language, be patient as confidence grows over time, be authentic, and consider cultural context in communication, especially if English is not your first language.

Verbal Communication involves using words to convey information, encompassing both speaking and writing. It is a two-way process where the sender and receiver play equally important roles. Effective verbal communication entails skills such as speaking clearly, listening actively, and considering non-verbal cues like body language and tone. First impressions matter and can influence subsequent conversations. Speaking effectively involves word choice, tone, and body language, all of which impact how your message is perceived. Active listening is crucial for meaningful communication. Advanced techniques like reinforcement, reflection, clarification, and questioning can enhance verbal communication. How you conclude a conversation can leave a lasting impression. Verbal and Non-verbal signals help in gracefully ending a conversation. Overall, improving verbal communication skills is vital for effective communication.

Non-verbal Communication, a critical aspect of human interaction, goes beyond words and includes body language, facial expressions, tone of voice, and personal space. It plays a pivotal role in conveying messages, expressing emotions, and establishing relationships. While non-verbal cues are essential in communication, they can vary greatly across cultures and situations. This form of communication is like an ever-changing language, and its interpretation depends on context and cultural norms. Additionally, non-verbal communication is not limited to face-to-face encounters; it can also manifest in written text through elements like handwriting and typography. Understanding the types of non-verbal communication, from body movements to physiological changes, is vital for effective inter-personal communication and cultural sensitivity.

Public Speaking skills have become increasingly valuable in today's fast-paced world, offering a plethora of benefits in education, politics, business, and daily life. This art of effective oral communication with an audience is not confined to formal speeches but extends to everyday interactions. It involves mastering the seven essential elements of the speaker, the message, the audience, the channel, feedback, noise, and the situation. By understanding and applying these elements, individuals can improve their public speaking abilities, boosting their confidence, communication skills, and career prospects. Additionally, public speaking encompasses various types, including ceremonial, demonstrative, informative, and persuasive speaking, each serving unique purposes in different contexts. Developing effective public speaking skills involves preparing thoroughly, understanding your audience, organizing your material, using humor and effective language, avoiding reading scripts, using voice and body language effectively, and making strong openings and closings. Overall, public speaking is a versatile skill that not only opens doors to success but also contributes to personal growth and the ability to influence and inspire others.

Extemporaneous Speech is when you talk in front of people without planning it beforehand. You get the topic just before you speak and have to think quickly. This type of speaking is often used to see if you can talk well about current events without getting ready in advance. It is flexible, sounds natural, helps with clear communication, makes you think fast, and boosts your confidence. When you are good at it, you sound calm and trustworthy, and you can even add recent stories or examples to keep your speech interesting. That is why extempore speaking is a great skill to have.

Group Discussion is like a formal talk where people discuss a special topic in a group. It helps see how well they talk, work together, and understand different ideas. It is all about sharing thoughts and listening to each other. In the classroom, teachers and students use group discussion to learn together. It is a good thing because students can share their ideas, work as a team, become more confident, and stop being shy. There are different ways to do group discussion, like talking about a chosen topic, debating, or having a friendly chat. Each way helps students learn and think. Group discussions can be planned or not, and they make the classroom more fun and interesting. But sometimes, not everyone gets to talk, people can feel pressured to agree, the talk can get messy, there can be arguments, and not enough time to say everything. So, while group discussions have lots of good things, they can also have some problems.

Barriers to Speaking Skills can include a lack of confidence, being too reserved, limited vocabulary, pronunciation issues, speaking too quickly, grammar challenges, lack of practice, inadequate use of gestures, and an unfavourable environment. Overcoming these barriers involves talking to others, seeking help from teachers and classmates, practicing regularly, using engaging stories, not fearing mistakes, and learning from skilled speakers to improve your speaking skills. Remember that speaking is a skill that can be developed over time with dedication and practice.

Questions

1. What is speaking?
2. Define speaking skills.
3. Discuss the features of speaking skills.
4. Point out the importance of speaking skills.

5. Discuss different types of speaking skills with suitable examples.
6. What is meant by effective speaking?
7. How can speaking be made effective?
8. Why is effective speaking important?
9. Discuss in detail about verbal communication.
10. Discuss in detail about non-verbal communication.
11. Write a short note on extempore.
12. Write a short note on public speaking.
13. What is group discussion? Discuss its types, advantages, and limitations in the teaching-learning perspective.
14. Discuss the barriers to speaking skills and how to overcome them.

Bibliography

6 barriers to speaking. https://www.ewriter29.com/skills/communication-skills/barriers-to-speaking/amp/

Bek Galloway. (2016, October 1). *Identify Purpose and Audience.* [Video]. YouTube. https:// www.youtube.com/watch?v=VrD9-In6C1o

Communication skill. https://slideplayer.com/amp/13574133/

Communication skill. https://www.slideshare.net/prakasraja/communication-skills-ppt

Curriculum and guidelines for life skills (Jeevan Kaushal)2.0, August,2023 by UGC, New Delhi, India.

Listening Skills. https://www.google.com/url?sa=t&source=web&rct=j&opi=89978449&url=

Mrinalini, T. & Ramakrishna, A. (2020). *Information and Communication Technology (ICT) in Education.* Neelkamal Publications Private Limited, New Delhi.

Mukhopadhyay, M. (2022). *Educational Technology for Teachers.* Shipra Publications, New Delhi.

Seven simple ways to improve your speaking skills, British Council. https://www.britishcouncil.in/blog/seven-simple-ways-improve-your-speaking-skills

Skills You Need (n.d.). *Barriers to Effective Listening. Skills You Need.* https://www. skillsyouneed.com/ips/ineffective-listening.html

Team Learn Pick. (n.d.). 8 Common Mistakes We Make While Speaking English. Learn Pick. https://www.learnpick.in/blog/8-common-mistakes-make-speaking-english

What are speaking skills? https://www.twinkl.co.in/teaching-wiki/speaking-skills

Index